TEN WAYS to BUILD a BRILLIANT BRAIN

ACKNOWLEDGEMENTS

I've learnt so much from all the brains I've ever met. For this book, I'm especially grateful for the brilliant questions from Year 7 and Year 8 students of Stockport School, Manchester, England, and their enthusiastic teacher, Karen Barber. Some questions are answered in the book but others were far too difficult for my brain. I can only hope that some of the students will become neuroscientists or philosophers so they can tell me their answers.

First published 2022 by Walker Books Ltd,
87 Vauxhall Walk, London SE11 5HJ

10 9 8 7 6 5 4 3 2 1

Text © 2022 Nicola Morgan

Illustrations © 2022 Risa Rodil

The right of Nicola Morgan and Risa Rodil
to be identified as author and illustrator
respectively of this work has been asserted
in accordance with the Copyright, Designs and
Patents Act 1988.

This book has been typeset in Futura

Printed in Italy

British Library Cataloguing in Publication Data: a catalogue
record for this book is available from the British Library

ISBN 978-1-4063-9541-9

www.walker.co.uk

CONTENTS

MEET YOUR BRAIN — 4

ONE — 17
GROW BRAIN CONNECTIONS

TWO — 35
FUEL YOUR BRAIN

THREE — 51
BE ACTIVE

FOUR — 63
SLEEP WELL

FIVE — 81
MAKE FRIENDS

SIX — 101
BOUNCE BACK

SEVEN — 117
BE CURIOUS

EIGHT — 129
BE CREATIVE

NINE — 145
LOVE BOOKS

TEN — 161
TAKE BREAKS

MEET YOUR BRAIN

Ten Ways to Build a Brilliant Brain shows you how to make your brain the best it can be.

Your brain is only a wet, soft lump of matter inside your skull but it gives you the power to do, think, feel, succeed and be a wonderful human being. It's already pretty brilliant!

WHICH OF THESE DOES YOUR BRAIN LET YOU DO ALREADY?

move, see, taste, smell, hear,
feel, love, dream, hope, make friends,
listen to music, create art, make plans,
design a poster, decorate a notebook, write, type,
use cutlery, make things, play musical instruments,
dance, jump, run, catch, kick, bend,
do a handstand, use a computer, read and
create stories, dream big ideas,
remember some facts,
remember your past

Your brain will learn even more in the future. This book will show you fun ways to make learning all that knowledge and those skills easier.

Throughout your life you will have countless choices. Sometimes you'll make the wrong choice and sometimes the right choice. This book will give you the knowledge to help you make good choices. But don't worry when you get something wrong: try again and bit by bit you'll push your brilliant brain in the right direction. Long journeys start with small steps.

In this book, look out for:

BRILLIANT BRAIN FACTS – Things to amaze your friends and family with.

BRILLIANT BRAIN BOOSTS – Things which will boost your brainpower and make you feel good now.

QUESTIONS FROM YOU – Questions that young people have asked me.

BRILLIANT BRAIN BOOST

Get a notebook for all the activities in this book and write down all the facts you learn. Give it a title. Maybe "My Brilliant Brain Book"? Decorate it however you want to.

YOUR BRAIN IS YOU

Inside your brain is everything that makes you you. Legs, eyes and ears are important, but you'd still be you without them.

In your brain are all your memories, skills, thoughts, emotions, hopes, dreams, likes and dislikes. When you say "I think", "I feel" or "I like", that's from your brain. It is you.

YOUR BRAIN NEEDS YOU

Your brain will be with you for your whole life so you want it to work as well as possible. When your brain works well, you feel better, and when you feel better it's easier to succeed at your goals. Luckily, some simple actions help your brain work well. There are things to avoid, too. This book will tell you them all.

Only you can look after your brain. Adults can help but the choices and actions will be yours. Can you rise to that challenge? Yes, you can! That's why you're reading this book!

BRILLIANT BRAIN BOOST

We learn more easily when we're happy and excited. And the words we use can affect what we think and believe. So, say out loud: "I'm happy and excited because reading this book is going to make my brain better." Say it a few times. Say it with confidence!

Like a coach before a match, give yourself a pep talk before you tackle a new task. When you wake up each day, tell yourself, "Today is a new day for my brain. Let's see what I can learn."

Write down three things you can't do yet that you'd love to be able to do one day. What will you need to achieve them? Any skills you'll need to practise? Determination? Luck? Support from other people? All of those things? Use these to take steps towards your goals.

DOES THIS BOOK WORK FOR EVERY BRAIN?

Human brains have lots of things that are the same and lots that are different. But there are some more significant differences: when someone has any of these they are described as "neurodiverse" or "neurodivergent", which is usually a better word. When someone does not have extra differences we say they are "neurotypical".

How can you tell if you are neurodivergent? A person is described as neurodivergent if there is a common skill that they find especially difficult, even when they have good teaching and try hard. If you find it extremely hard to do one or more things that most of your friends find quite easy, you could have a neurodivergent brain.

It's useful to know this because there are ways to get help. Maybe you need a different teaching method. Or more time or support. Once you see that human brains operate in a variety of ways, you can start to understand and respect your own brain and help it do a great job for you.

Neurodivergent brains can also have powerful abilities. For example, someone might struggle to read or spell but have an exceptional memory or draw amazing pictures or do complicated mental maths.

So, we're all different, but neurodivergent people have extra difference, which makes some aspects of life difficult but sometimes gives an advantage. Here are some common examples of neurodivergence:

- Dyslexia – difficulty with aspects of reading or writing
- Dyspraxia – difficulty with hand-writing, tying shoelaces, and organising and planning ahead
- Autistic Spectrum Condition or ASC – difficulty in knowing how to understand or react to others; anxiety at change of routine; strong reactions to noise, light or touch
- ADHD/ADD (Attention Deficit Hyperactivity Disorder or Attention Deficit Disorder) – difficulty concentrating or sitting quietly

Everything in this book applies to every brain. Everyone can use all the ten ways to build a brilliant brain!

QUESTION FROM YOU

ALEXUS ASKED

WHY DO WE NEED OUR BRAIN?

Your brain allows you to do everything you do! There is literally nothing that you can do or think or feel without your brain.

BRILLIANT BRAIN BASICS

There are fascinating things to know about the 1.5kg lump of stuff inside your head! Learning facts is useful but also fun.

HUMAN BRAINS: THE SAME AND DIFFERENT

Human brains are all **wired** for human behaviours. The parts of our brains used for speech and language are very well developed, allowing us to think, communicate, create and empathise.

Each human brain is also unique. Even identical twins don't have identical brains. They are more alike than any other people, but they have different experiences and thoughts, and those things make them different.

Understanding that we are all the same and different is very important. You are human but also you: unique.

BRILLIANT BRAIN FACT

Any word that begins with neuro or neur is to do with the brain. Neuroscience is the science of the brain. You can guess what neurosurgery is!

ONE BRILLIANT BRAIN: ALBERT EINSTEIN

Albert Einstein was one of the cleverest scientists who ever lived. He had ideas no one had thought of. After his death, his brain was stolen by Dr Thomas Harvey, who photographed it and cut it into 240 pieces for examination by himself and later scientists.

Some found possible small differences between Einstein's brain and average brains. But it's difficult to be sure. Einstein had been dead many years when his brain was examined, and it was stored badly. (Some say it was kept in a cider-barrel!) And no one compared his brain to other clever thinkers to see if they had the same physical differences.

It is just not possible to know whether Einstein's brain had a visible difference that could explain his exceptional thinking skills, or whether his cleverness was because of how he used his brain. Or maybe the way he used his brain created any physical differences that might have existed.

BRAINY WORDS

You'll find a glossary of important words on page 176. Throughout the book, any word in the glossary will be in bold.

MOST IMPORTANT BRAIN PARTS

Different parts of your brain are responsible for each of the different things you do.

Prefrontal cortex

Just behind your forehead. It's often called the "control" centre. We use it when making sensible decisions, working things out and controlling our impulses. It's very well-developed in humans compared to other animals.

Amygdala

Have you heard of "fight, flight or freeze"? It's also called the "stress response". This happens in the amygdala, when the brain detects a threat. In ancient humans, the amygdala kept us alert to dangers like lions or snakes or enemies. Nowadays, most of us have different threats: exams, performance, dealing with criticism or worries, arguments with other people, pressure to succeed. Sometimes our amygdala is too active and we feel stressed or anxious too often or too much. In Chapter Ten, you'll learn how to avoid the problems of stress.

Hippocampus

New information or experiences are **processed** first in your hippocampus. Then, if you keep trying to remember the information, it goes to other areas to be stored in long-term memory.

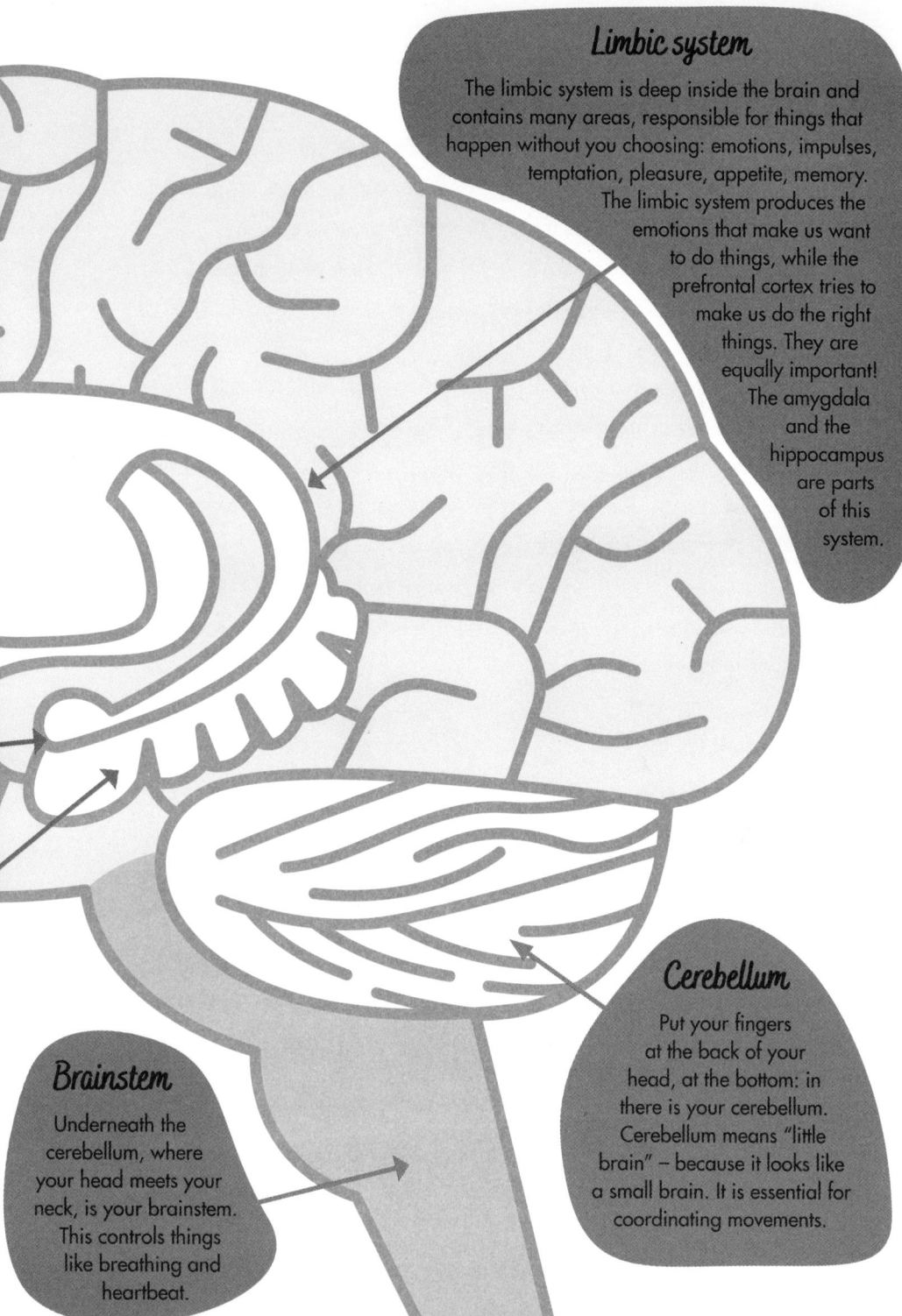

Limbic system

The limbic system is deep inside the brain and contains many areas, responsible for things that happen without you choosing: emotions, impulses, temptation, pleasure, appetite, memory. The limbic system produces the emotions that make us want to do things, while the prefrontal cortex tries to make us do the right things. They are equally important! The amygdala and the hippocampus are parts of this system.

Cerebellum

Put your fingers at the back of your head, at the bottom: in there is your cerebellum. Cerebellum means "little brain" – because it looks like a small brain. It is essential for coordinating movements.

Brainstem

Underneath the cerebellum, where your head meets your neck, is your brainstem. This controls things like breathing and heartbeat.

YOUR LEFT AND RIGHT HEMISPHERES

Your brain is split into two halves, called hemispheres. Your left brain hemisphere controls the right side of your body, and vice-versa. Each side of your body (eye, ear, nostril, skin, fingers) takes in information separately and processes it on the opposite side of the brain.

Each hemisphere is similar but not identical, with almost every brain part appearing on both sides. You have two amygdalae and hippocampi, for example. But each hemisphere is slightly different in size and shape. And some activities happen more on one side than the other, or slightly differently on one side.

For example, in *most* people language is processed mainly in the left hemisphere. But the information moves so quickly between the sides that you are really using both hemispheres all the time, whatever you are doing. You can't choose!

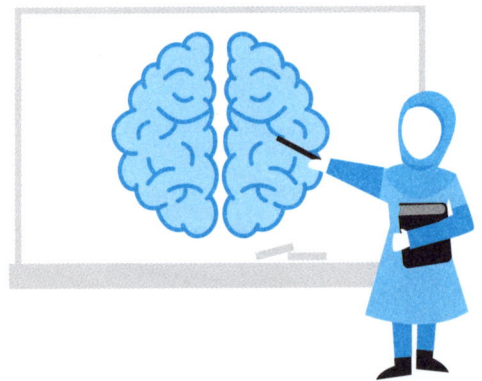

BRILLIANT BRAIN FACT

You can have an operation on your brain and be awake during it without feeling pain. Your skull feels pain (so you'd have an anaesthetic for when the surgeon drills through) but your actual brain has no pain sensors.

WHY DO WE GET HEADACHES?

Although brains can't feel pain, the parts between your brain and your skull can. Headaches can be caused by tiredness, or eye strain, or not eating or drinking enough, stress, fever or illnesses such as colds or flu. Such headaches are very common and usually harmless.

Headaches are occasionally serious. If your headache is accompanied by any of the following, tell an adult immediately: a recent injury to head or neck, feeling ill or vomiting, difficulty or pain moving your neck.

KEEP YOUR BRAIN SAFE

Your brain is precious! You can't live without it and it can't be replaced. "Brain damage" involves damaged cells and connections. If this happens, the patient won't be able (or will find it harder) to do whatever the damaged areas were responsible for. So, if someone damages the networks for moving their right foot, they'll have a problem moving their right foot. If someone damages the networks for the ability to recognise faces, they'll have trouble recognising faces.

Often a patient can get lost skills back, usually with the help of a physiotherapist. This is easier for young people than adults.

TIPS TO PROTECT YOUR BRILLIANT BRAIN

1. Wear a helmet for cycling, climbing, skateboarding and sports where a hard ball is thrown (such as cricket or baseball).

2. Never buy a second-hand helmet; if yours gets a bad knock, replace it. This might be expensive but it's your life and health.

3. Don't play contact sports with players of a very different size or weight. Use official clubs with good coaching and supervision. If you hit your head, tell an adult.

4. Avoid "heading" in football. In some countries this is banned at youth level, because repeated knocks can cause damage.

5. Look after the health of your heart and blood system by doing regular exercise and making good food choices.

6. Avoid alcohol, drugs and "legal highs".

WHAT YOU'VE LEARNT

You've learnt fascinating facts about typical brains and unusual brains. You've seen how human brains are the same in some ways but also different, making each of us unique.

Your brain is in your head but I say that it's also "in your hands", because there's so much you can do to make it work brilliantly. That's what the rest of this book is about.

Let's look at the first of the ten ways to build your brilliant brain.

ONE

GROW BRAIN CONNECTIONS

THE MAIN MESSAGE

To learn anything and become good at it, you need to connect lots of neurons – the nerve cells in your brain and spine – into networks. This chapter will show you how to build lots of strong connections between your neurons so your brain can become more brilliant!

WHAT YOU NEED TO KNOW

YOUR PLASTIC BRAIN

Scientists describe brains as "plastic". This means that your brain physically changes with each new thing you learn or experience, like modelling dough that can always be reshaped. The brain of someone who plays the piano every day or reads books a lot will be different from the brain of someone who doesn't.

This is because every mental or physical action builds or strengthens connections between nerve cells, called **neurons**. And every type of activity that you don't do means that some connections aren't built or strengthened.

Suppose you play computer games for two hours a day during a holiday. And supposing during that holiday you don't read books or practise keepy-uppies. You'd grow and strengthen lots of connections to do with playing computer games. But what about the connections you had already built for reading or keepy-uppies? They would become weaker. You'd become less good at those things. You'd need to practise them again! Then your plastic brain would regrow the connections.

Every day, you do thousands of actions, think thousands of thoughts and have thousands of experiences. Each one changes your brain a tiny bit. Your brain is even changing as you read this.

My words are rewiring your brain!

You have been rewiring your plastic brain since you were born; each year you've built many skills.

This applies to everything:

🧪 Physical actions such as tying shoelaces, kicking a ball, playing the drums and drawing a picture.

🧪 Mental actions such as learning that the capital of France is Paris, remembering something you did, doing mental maths and using your imagination.

Each time you practise, you make connections between neurons. You change your brain every time.

QUESTION FROM YOU

HOW DOES THE BRAIN HELP US LEARN THINGS?

The short answer is: by making connections between neurons so messages can pass quickly along networks. The rest of the answer is what this chapter is about!

RACHAEL ASKED

GROWTH AND FIXED MINDSETS

A **mindset** is a set of beliefs. Your mindsets are formed by the people around you, the things that have happened to you and the thoughts you have. And your mindsets can change.

One mindset is to do with whether you think that strengths and weaknesses are just a matter of luck, or whether you think you can do anything about them. Are you "good at" this or that mostly because you were born that way or because of your actions?

A growth mindset says, "If I want to be good at things, I need to have good teaching, practise hard and be determined. If I take the right steps, I'll get there. I can gradually build my skills; my success is largely in my own hands."

A fixed mindset is the opposite, saying, "The things I'm good or bad at are my natural skills or weaknesses. They just are how they are and won't change."

A growth mindset gives you more belief in your future and more control over your success. This isn't the same as believing you can do anything. No one can do everything. But believing you can do a lot helps you stay motivated and determined and that's the surest way to success.

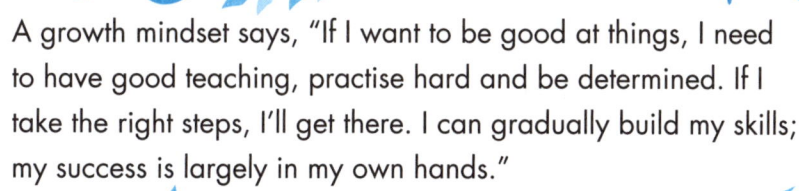

BRILLIANT BRAIN BOOST

Write down five things you couldn't do when you were two years old that you can do now. Write down five things you'd like to be able to do when you're older. For each one, write down something you'll need to do to achieve it. Then decide which one you'll try first. Make a start!

MINDSET QUIZ

Let's see whether your mindset is currently more growth or fixed! (And remember: it can change.) Read these statements and decide which you agree with most strongly in each group.

1. When I make a mistake...

A. When I make a mistake, I get upset and feel I'll never succeed. I should stick to what I'm good at!

B. When I make a mistake, I feel upset but I quickly put it behind me and it makes me more determined to try again.

C. When I make a mistake, I don't care! It's just not my skill and it doesn't bother me.

2. The people in my class

A. When people are better than me at something it's because they naturally have talent.

B. When people are better than me at something it's because their parents give them encouragement and support.

C. When people do better than me at something it's for a variety of reasons but all that matters is that I can improve if I work hard.

3. Getting feedback from someone

A. I think it's best if the person focuses on my good points and just gives me praise.

B. I don't really notice praise, only the negative criticism.

C. Obviously praise is nice but I want to improve so I prefer to be told what I did wrong.

4. Wishes or hopes

A. I wish I had more time and energy to practise all the things I'd love to be good at!

B. I wish I was naturally talented so everything would be easy.

C. I wish I had more determination and willpower to keep practising but too often I give up.

5. My future

A. I think my future is in my hands. Although setbacks will happen, there will be masses of opportunities. I just need to look for them.

B. I don't think I'll have an amazing future because I have a lot of problems, so I need to be satisfied with whatever comes.

C. I'm very positive about my future because I'm generally really lucky so loads of opportunities will come.

6. Perfection

A. If I can't do something really well, it's sensible to keep trying for a bit but then give up and try something else.

B. If I can't do something really well, it's because I don't have that particular talent, so there's no point in trying to be better.

C. If I can't do something really well, it's because I haven't yet built the skills I need. If I keep trying, I'll improve.

7. Easy things

A. When something is easy, I am happy because I won't have to work hard! I'll stick to that level and feel satisfied.

B. When something is easy, it's boring so I like to move to a harder level.

C. When something is easy, I feel proud of how clever I am.

WORKING OUT YOUR SCORE

Each statement has one "best" answer, which scores 3 and suggests a growth mindset. There are also some differences between the other answers: some score 0 (indicating a fixed mindset) and some score 1 (indicating a slightly fixed mindset with some signs of growth to build on).

1. A: 0   B: 3   C: 0
2. A: 0   B: 1   C: 3
3. A: 0   B: 0   C: 3
4. A: 3   B: 0   C: 1
5. A: 3   B: 0   C: 1
6. A: 1   B: 0   C: 3
7. A: 0   B: 3   C: 1

WHAT YOUR SCORE MEANS

14–21 – You have a strong growth mindset! You believe that your best chance of success is by working hard, listening well and practising the skills you want.

7–13 – As you fall in the middle, take a look at which questions you scored a 0 or 1 and which a 3. You did have at least one growth mindset answer, which is great. See if you can build on that in your life, by working on one of the growth mindset answers at a time.

0–6 – Your answers suggest a fixed mindset which could be holding you back, but you can change this. You don't have to do it on your own. Adults can help you: ask them how you can build your confidence. Schools are supposed to boost growth mindset, so talk to your teachers.

This chapter is giving you more of a growth mindset because you're learning that you get better at things by trying. Now let's see how you can put this into action!

   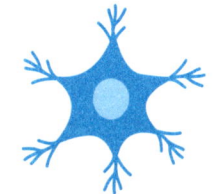

HOW TO USE THIS KNOWLEDGE

Now that you understand the need to grow connections in your brain, how can you make it happen? I have lots of ideas. The more of them you try, the more your brain will learn and improve.

HOW TO GROW CONNECTIONS

You've been doing this without thinking, ever since you were born. But once you see how, you'll feel more in control. I love thinking about my brain actually growing connections!

Use these tips to grow your connections.

Try and try again

This works for every sort of learning: facts, spellings, vocabulary, maths, music, and all the physical skills involved in sports, art and making things. Every time you try, you grow and strengthen connections.

BRILLIANT BRAIN BOOST

Watch closely when your teacher or coach shows you how to do something. Imagine yourself doing it and think about it carefully. Your brain is making networks for you while you just watch!

There's no such thing as being right-brained or left-brained. Some activities do use the right hemisphere more – such as creativity, daydreaming, processing things from the external world – and some things use the left more – such as speaking. (Although there are some differences, with some people using the other side for language, for example.) But both hemispheres work brilliantly together all the time. If you spend a lot of time doing art, for example, you are using your right brain a lot, but this does not mean you are right-brained or that the right side of your brain is "dominant".

Watch someone else

This works best for physical skills such as for gymnastics or dance, sport or playing an instrument. When you watch someone do something, special neurons called mirror neurons become active, starting to grow branches called **dendrites** and build connections.

When you try the action yourself, it will be a tiny bit easier than if you'd never watched. Your brain behaves as though you've already done it!

Practise correctly!

This works for everything, too. Imagine you're learning spellings and one is written down wrongly. Seeing the wrong spelling a few times could mean you'll wire the wrong spelling into your brain and have to spend effort rewiring it.

Here are some tips to practise correctly:

❋ Take care when writing information down. If you aren't sure it's correct, check.

❋ If you feel you might be doing something wrong, ask someone to show you again.

❋ Take special care to ask for help if it's something you quite often get muddled.

If you discover you've been learning anything wrong, commit extra time to learning the correct version. Write it down and pin it where you'll see it often. Test yourself daily until you get it right. Little by little, you'll rewire your brain.

BRILLIANT BRAIN BOOST

When you think "I can't do this" or "This is too hard", always remember that the more you try the better you'll get. Each time, imagine the brain networks you are building.

Daydream and mind-wander

This works well for processing information, solving problems or having creative ideas.

Try this after school, maybe on your way home. Letting your mind wander gives your brain a chance to grow connections for whatever you've been working on. People too often get a phone out and focus on that. It fills their brain with information and doesn't let them process what they just learnt. Here are some ideas:

Look out of the window, whether on a bus, in a car, or in your bedroom

Go for a walk

Do anything that occupies your hands but not much of your mind, like knitting, doodling, stroking a pet

Tidy your room or desk

BRILLIANT BRAIN BOOST

If you have a phone, leave it in your pocket when you're on your way home from school. That gives you valuable mind-wandering time.

Exercise

Physical activity helps the brain build new connections. Try walking, kicking a ball, tree-climbing or whatever you like.

Sleep

During sleep, your brain grows and strengthens connections for whatever you were doing during the day. You'll find more about how sleep helps you build a brilliant brain in Chapter Four.

BRILLIANT BRAIN FACT

When you were born, your brain contained 85–100 billion neurons. Humans start losing neurons from our thirties so you probably have more than I do. But the number of neurons isn't what's important: it's all the strong connections between neurons that makes a brain able to do things.

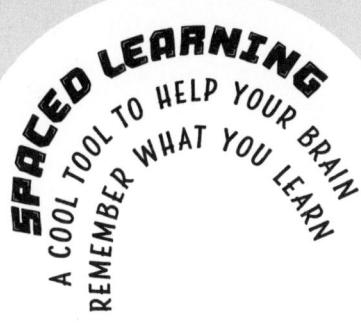

SPACED LEARNING
A COOL TOOL TO HELP YOUR BRAIN REMEMBER WHAT YOU LEARN

Suppose you're trying to learn for a test. Maybe spelling or vocabulary. Or maybe you're performing in a play and you have to learn some words. Here's a tip: try spaced learning! The trick is not to try to do it all in one session. Information quickly fades if we don't keep repeating it. One long session is never as useful as several shorter ones.

Spaced learning also involves making the gaps between practice sessions start small and get longer. Whatever you are trying to learn and however much time you have, you can work out a schedule so that the spaces between practice sessions get longer. Plan to have at least five sessions. Whether you have two days or two months to learn something, spacing your practice sessions like this helps the information stick in your long-term memory.

GROW A GROWTH MINDSET

You learnt about growth mindset on page 20. Here's how to improve yours:

1. Re-read the beginning of this chapter to remind yourself that we learn by practising, and every practice helps us grow new connections and become a tiny bit better.

2. Remind yourself how much you've already learnt. Write down twenty things – facts or skills – you've learnt since you were born. You will learn more and more things, just by trying.

3. Ask your parents to praise effort, not talent. When you do well, they should say "Well done – you succeeded because you worked hard!" Not "Well done – you succeeded because you're so talented!"

4. Value each small achievement; don't wait for perfection. Be proud that you learnt one more spelling than last week, rather than fretting that you didn't get them all right.

BRILLIANT BRAIN BOOST

Feel proud: you've built a brilliant growth mindset! Be positive because it will help you for your whole life.

QUIZ FOR THIS CHAPTER

1. What does "my brain is plastic" mean?

A. My brain will take hundreds of years to decompose.

B. My brain changes with everything I do and everything that happens to it.

C. My brain is hard, like a plastic model.

2. How do you grow connections between neurons?

A. By trying and practising different skills.

B. By waiting until you are old enough to be really good at things.

C. By staying awake as long as possible.

3. "Use it or lose it" means:

A. If you aren't careful, you will lose things.

B. If you don't practise the things you've built neural networks for, you will lose connections in those areas and lose some skills.

C. If you don't use your brain, it will disappear.

4. Spaced learning means:

A. Learning about planets and stars.

B. Learning in a comfortable space.

C. Spacing learning sessions with increasing gaps between them.

5. What does a growth mindset mean?

A. When a person's mind grows bigger the more they think.

B. When a person believes they can grow any skills they choose by working hard and practising well.

C. When a person believes they have certain talents and abilities because of luck.

Answers at the bottom of the page

WHAT YOU'VE LEARNT

You've learnt how to grow a growth mindset! You know a lot about how brains change as we practise skills or try to learn and remember things. And you've discovered some practical ways to help your brain learn better and more easily. That's what everyone wants!

Knowing this isn't enough, though. You have to put it into practice and take care of your brain. Are you up for the challenge of building the best brain you can? All the next chapters will show you how.

Answers 1.B 2.A 3.B 4.C 5.B

TWO

FUEL YOUR BRAIN

THE MAIN MESSAGE

Humans need energy, which comes from food and drink. Your brain uses lots of energy. If it doesn't get enough, it can't do the best job for you.

WHAT YOU NEED TO KNOW

ENERGY AND YOUR BRAIN

The brain needs a lot of energy. It's only around two per cent of your body weight but uses around twenty per cent of the fuel (food and drink) you consume. That's because it has many jobs, which all use energy. For example, as well as your mental and physical actions, your brain regulates breathing and heart activity. Even sleeping brains burn energy!

If your brain doesn't get enough energy, you'll feel tired and find it hard to concentrate. You won't be able to do your best work.

Getting energy is usually easy: you just eat enough food. And that food needs to have two things: calories and nutrients.

ENERGY AND CALORIES

Energy in food is measured as calories. You need enough calories each day. Otherwise, you might feel dizzy or light-headed; you might get headaches; and it will be difficult to concentrate. Being hungry is the first sign that you need more calories.

Different foods produce different amounts of energy. A "high-calorie" food produces a lot of energy compared to a "low-calorie" food. It's better to call it high-energy or low-energy food.

Lettuce and cucumber are low-energy. You'd have to eat a lot of them before they'd give you enough energy.

Nuts and cake are high-energy. Nuts are usually a better choice (if you aren't allergic to them) because:

- Their energy lasts longer because the calories in cake are mostly from sugar, which the body processes very quickly.

- Nuts contain lots of nutrients, whereas most cake doesn't contain many. (But some cakes have nuts, fruit and seeds, making them a better choice.)

You will find loads more examples of good energy-giving food choices on page 43.

NUTRIENTS

All foods contain different nutrients, each of which does different jobs.

Getting the right nutrients is much easier than you might think, because you don't have to know what nutrients are in each food. All you need to do is eat a wide variety of foods and you will get all the nutrients you need. You'll find great ideas on the next pages!

37

ARE THERE SUPER BRAIN FOODS?

There are many claims that certain foods are "superfoods" that have special brain benefits. Blueberries, broccoli and Brazil nuts are examples of foods that some people call superfoods.

Be careful. Even if a food is nutritious, as those examples are, it might be unhealthy to have a lot of it. And if you have too much of one thing you might not eat enough of another. Blueberries, broccoli and nuts are brilliant foods but so are lots of other things. Variety is the key.

DO FOOD SUPPLEMENTS WORK?

Buying expensive tablets, liquids or powders in a pharmacy or health food store is not the best way of getting nutrients. Supplements sometimes have claims that have not been fully tested. For example, vitamin pills might promise to keep your brain in top condition. All that means is that they contain nutrients which are good for brains. But so does a varied diet and there's no proof that pills would do a better job. It's likely that they wouldn't.

If a doctor or qualified dietitian recommends you take a supplement, that's fine, of course.

IS SUGAR GOOD OR BAD?

No food is "bad" but some foods should have a smaller part in your diet than others. Here are some facts about sugar:

IMPORTANT NOTE ABOUT DIABETES

People with diabetes react differently to sugar and this advice is not intended for anyone with this illness. If you have diabetes, only follow food advice from your doctors, not from this book. That's very important.

- There are many forms of sugar with different names – for example, fructose, sucrose and glucose. You'll see these in ingredient lists on food packets.

- Sugar is found naturally in many foods, including all fruit and vegetables and rice, pasta, potatoes and bread.

- Sugary foods and drinks can lead to tooth decay if we don't clean our teeth properly.

- The more sugary foods we eat, the more likely we are to "crave" sugar and eat more than is healthy.

- Our body turns all the sugar we eat into glucose and then into energy.

39

BLOOD SUGAR LEVELS

If you aren't eating properly, the level of glucose in your body and brain will drop. You might feel light-headed or faint and maybe get a headache. You'll struggle to concentrate or achieve your best, mentally and physically. You'll be like a machine that's running out of battery.

If you eat something very sugary, you get a fast energy boost, but your glucose levels will drop quickly. This doesn't feel good and it isn't the best way to fuel your brain.

So, some sugar is important. But eating too much sugary food isn't a good way to fuel brain or body. And too much sugar over a long period can cause problems such as diabetes.

A NOTE ON ARTIFICIAL SWEETENERS

When something says "sugar free" or "no added sugar", it will often contain artificial sweetener. This applies to foods, drinks, chewing gum and medicines. Because they don't have any calories, artificial sweeteners can't fuel your brain! So although they might not harm you, they aren't giving you a benefit.

BRILLIANT BRAIN FACT

You might have heard that special "energy" drinks can keep your brain alert. But they are only recommended for people doing extreme levels of sport or at times when they can't eat. For everyone else they are not a good idea. They will make your blood sugar go up and down and can make you feel unwell. The caffeine in energy drinks can be addictive and affect sleep.

WATER AND THE BRAIN

Water has no calories so doesn't provide energy. But it's essential for body and brain. The brain is over 70 per cent water, after all. Water keeps your brain and body healthy and helps you feel comfortable.

Any liquid is mostly water so things like diluted juice or cordial or herbal tea also help keep you hydrated. It is better to have mostly water, though. The following drinks are not good for keeping your fluid levels up:

- Cola and any fizzy drinks
- Very sugary drinks
- Drinks with caffeine in

You'll find practical tips for how to get enough water in your diet on page 48.

QUESTION FROM YOU

MAX & MILLIE ASKED

WHAT IS THE BRAIN MADE OF? WHAT COLOUR IS IT?

A living brain is soft and is mostly fat, protein and water. There is "grey matter" and "white matter". The white matter comes from a very important fat called myelin that coats parts of the neurons. The rest of the neurons are the grey matter. Blood vessels add a slightly pinky colour. So it's a combination of grey, white and pink.

HOW TO USE THIS KNOWLEDGE

Most people work best on three main meals a day: breakfast, lunch and a meal in the evening (not too close to bedtime). You might get hungry between meals, too, especially if you're being very active. It's good to have a snack if you're hungry, but try to make choices that will fuel your brain and body well. This section has lots of tips and ideas.

WHAT DO YOU ALREADY EAT?

If you look at what you eat on a typical day, that will help you see what you might be missing. So, look at yesterday or pick a different day if that was more typical. Then look at the list on the opposite page.

How many portions of those did you eat? Did you eat at least ten different items from among them? For example, baked beans on wholemeal toast and a glass of milk would be three.

A portion would be very roughly equivalent to ten grapes, one apple or banana, eight mouthfuls of chicken or fish, a small yogurt, a couple of tablespoons of rice or vegetables or salad.

Don't worry about being exact but just be aware that one mouthful of something would not be a whole portion.

Eggs
Fish (fresh, frozen or tinned)
Chicken
Soya or tofu – for example, in vegetarian mince
Beans, peas, lentils
Hummus
Dairy food (milk, cheese or yogurt from cow, sheep or goat),
or alternatives to dairy milk (soya, almond or oat)
Oats (porridge or cereal, for example)
Wholegrain or wholemeal bread
Wholegrain cereal without lots of added sugar
Fruit other than berries
Berries
Dark green vegetables
Vegetables of other colours, including potatoes
Salad (lettuce, peppers, tomatoes)
Nuts
Seeds
Pasta or rice (ideally wholemeal/brown)

It's fine to eat foods that
are not on this list as well!
Just make sure *these* foods
feature often.

BRILLIANT BRAIN FOOD ON A BUDGET

Lots of nutritious foods are expensive and many families will worry about this. It's often the food you'll see in advertising that is the priciest.

But lots of wonderfully nutritious foods are not expensive. There are many cheaper options. A brilliant brain diet can be done on a tight budget.

- Oats are cheap, filling and nutritious. Try porridge for breakfast and oats in smoothies.

- Frozen fruit and vegetables are cheaper but just as healthy – they are frozen when very fresh. You can thaw just what you need. A frozen bag of berries can last several meals.

- Tinned food is often cheaper and just as nutritious. (Avoid tins with lots of added sugar and salt.)

- Supermarket basic ranges are often just as good as premium brands.

- Buy big bags when possible. You could share with another family.

- Making your own is usually cheaper. Try the recipe for Brain Bars on my website for healthy, brain-fuelling snacks.

HOW TO WIDEN YOUR DIET FOR A BRILLIANT BRAIN

Here are ideas to power your brain with a brilliant range of foods:

1. Be adventurous

Find foods you've never tried. Pick one and pledge to try it.
Here are some ideas:

Tinned sardines, mackerel or pilchards mashed up with mayo or cream cheese and squished onto toast.

Next time you eat out with family or friends, share a new dish with someone else so it doesn't matter if you don't like it.

Hummus – homemade is easy and cheap: find recipes online and add flavours such as lemon, pepper, parsley.

2. Be clever

- A spoonful of something you're not keen on doesn't have to spoil a meal. Mash it up and mix it in – you might not even taste it!

- If it's the texture you dislike, whizz it into a smoothie or soup.

- Eat the thing you don't like first. Then you'll feel proud and enjoy your meal. Soon you might LIKE the new food!

- Challenge yourself to eat a certain number of mouthfuls of whatever it is you want to like.

3. Be sociable

Collaborate with friends on a meal. Discuss in advance one thing you'll each make, so you get a variety. You can each make your dish at home (or pairing up) and come together to eat it. Beach, park or garden picnic, perhaps!

4. Learn to cook something

Cooking is a great way to develop your tastes. Here are some ideas:

Make my Brain Bars or Brain Cake – recipes on my website.

Perfect your own savoury rice. Cook rice according to the packet; stir-fry any of the following and add to the cooked rice: onion, pepper, mushroom, garlic, tomato. Add a few seeds, e.g. pumpkin or sunflower, and/or cashew nuts. Stir through some tinned tuna for a more filling meal.

Home-made pizza is surprisingly easy and usually cheaper and healthier than takeaway.

Try whizzing frozen fruit or vegetables into a smoothie, purée or soup. This is a great idea if you don't like it whole or lumpy!

WHAT TO DO IF THERE ARE FOODS YOU CAN'T EAT

If you avoid certain foods – perhaps because of an allergy or you are vegetarian or vegan – you have to be more informed so that you still get all the nutrients. Here are my top tips:

Discover what main nutrients are in the things you don't eat and find replacement foods you can eat.

Find the main organisation supporting your particular diet. They will have the best advice. If you have a very restricted diet, you might be advised to take some supplements.

WHAT TO DO IF YOU'RE ILL

Most illnesses take away your appetite. Don't worry about this: you're not using so much energy and you don't need the fuel. Just eat what you feel like when you feel ready. Try tiny portions or nibbles of the plainest food. Water is more important so do try to keep your fluid levels up.

HYDRATE YOUR BRILLIANT BRAIN

You know water is good for your brain. But how much should you drink, and what can you do if you find it boring?

Although coffee and tea are drinks that can keep you alert with caffeine, this can cause problems. They are less good than plain water at keeping you hydrated; they can make you too alert and jittery; and they make it harder to sleep at night. Avoid them completely in the evening.

48

How much:

- Drink enough that you don't feel thirsty. If you feel thirsty, drink more!
- Drink more in hot weather, during and after physical activity and if you are sweating.
- You'll sometimes read advice that you should drink at least eight glasses a day. This includes the water you'll get from food and other drinks, so don't be anxious about this – just avoid being thirsty.

If you think it's boring:

- Add ice or keep fresh water in the fridge.
- Flavour it with a piece of mint (which you can grow in a pot), or slice of cucumber or orange.
- Try herbal or fruit tea, which you can also chill until you want it.
- When working or reading, have water in front of you so you can't miss it.
- Drink a glass with every meal.
- When you drink, do it mindfully: notice that gorgeous cool water spreading down your throat.

QUIZ FOR THIS CHAPTER

1. How many calories are in a glass of plain water?

2. Which has a wider variety of nutrients: a piece of sponge cake or a handful of nuts?

3. Are frozen vegetables usually: a) as nutritious as fresh; b) less nutritious than fresh; c) more expensive than fresh?

4. Which TWO of these situations mean you should drink more water: a) When the weather is hot; b) When it's raining; c) When you've been exercising?

5. If caffeine helps keep you alert, why would experts not recommend it, especially for young brains?

Answers at the bottom of the page

WHAT YOU'VE LEARNT

Food fuels your body and brain and you need enough food to keep your calorie levels up so that you can work brilliantly. You won't do your best work when you're too hungry. Different foods have different nutrients and you need them all, so eat a wide variety, including as many different coloured fruits and veg as you can. You know that water doesn't fuel your brain, but it's still an essential part of your diet and if you don't have enough your brain won't work so well.

THREE

BE ACTIVE

THE MAIN MESSAGE
Physical activity strengthens your body but it also powers your brain, improving mental health and helping you learn. Being active is easier when you understand the benefits and when you find activities that you can really enjoy.

WHAT YOU NEED TO KNOW

WHAT HAPPENS IN YOUR BRAIN WHEN YOU EXERCISE?

1. **BLOOD CARRIES MORE OXYGEN AND GLUCOSE**
During physical activity, your lungs take in more oxygen and your heart pumps blood faster, giving brain and body more oxygen and glucose. So, although blood reaches your brain when you're sitting still, more passes through when you're active.

2. **YOU PRODUCE ENDORPHINS**
Endorphins are often called "happy chemicals". Just like some medicines, they help remove pain or distress. They are produced in the brain, not from food or medicine. Exercise triggers endorphins. Have you noticed how good you feel mentally after exercise, even if you didn't love doing it? That's endorphins. Things like running, football, tennis, basketball or walking up a hill might feel tough at the time but what a great feeling afterwards – once you've got your breath!

3. **YOU PRODUCE DOPAMINE**
Dopamine is a brain chemical that is incredibly motivating, making the brain keen to learn. I call it the YES chemical. Exercise makes the brain produce dopamine.

4. **YOU BUILD SKILLS**

As you know, when you practise you grow neural connections and get better at things. This is really obvious with physical skills. For example:

1. When you play football, you build neural networks that control your feet and coordination.
2. When you catch or hit a ball, you build networks that control muscles in your arms and coordination.
3. When you practise keepy-uppies, you build networks for balance, coordination and concentration.
4. On a climbing wall, you develop networks for planning and coordination.

5. **YOU CREATE NEW NEURONS**

Exercise can trigger the brain to create new neurons. The hippocampus is where this seems to happen most. That's the part which is most important for building new memories and learning. So, although you already have plenty of neurons, growing more in your hippocampus might be useful.

BRILLIANT BRAIN FACT

Babies can't form long-term memories until they are around three years old. At that time, changes happen in the hippocampus to allow these memories to form. This is why you can't remember anything earlier than that.

6. YOU PROCESS NEW LEARNING

When you've been working hard at schoolwork and can't take in any more, having a break and doing physical activity allows your brain to process what you've learnt. It does this by growing neural connections as well as moving information into long-term memory areas. (More about this in Chapter Ten.)

7. SELF-ESTEEM IMPROVES

If you're forced to do sport that you dislike or feel you're no good at, this can make you feel bad about yourself. But activity that you choose usually makes you feel better about yourself. Even just knowing that you did something healthy can boost your mood.

Feeling good about yourself helps mental health and makes your brain ready to learn. That feeling of "I did that" leads to "I can do this too". One positive feeling leads to another.

8. SLEEP IMPROVES

Exercise during the day helps you sleep well at night. Scientists aren't sure why but it's likely that exercise helps you feel relaxed and happy. When you feel bad about yourself or anxious and stressed, you sleep badly. So, feeling happy and relaxed helps you fall asleep. Always do your exercise during the day and just a few gentle stretches or yoga in the evening. Avoid raising your heart rate too close to sleep time.

HOW MUCH OF OUR BRAIN DO WE USE?

All of it! Just not all at the same time. You might have heard that you only use ten per cent of your brain. This is nonsense! There's no spare area which isn't used for something.

HOW MUCH EXERCISE SHOULD YOU DO?

A healthy person your age should aim to be active for at least an hour a day. This doesn't have to be all at once and does not mean you have to get sweaty by going for a run or playing sport: it just means moving about rather than sitting down. There are many easy ways of doing this, as you'll see in the next pages.

And it's definitely not a good idea to be obsessive about exercise: some people do too much and that's not healthy either.

Read on and you'll get a good sense of what is best for your brain as well as your body.

If you've been sitting down for an hour, get up and move around for a few minutes. Play with the dog, run round the block or walk up and down stairs.

FRESH AIR AND SUNLIGHT

Getting outside is important for body and brain, whatever the weather. If you spend a lot of time indoors with the windows shut and no air conditioning, the air you breathe will gradually have less oxygen in it. After a while you will find it harder to concentrate; you might also get a headache and feel groggy. When you can't go outside, opening a window or door helps refresh the air indoors. Fresh air is also good for dispersing germs.

You are more likely to catch other people's colds or other viruses indoors with the window shut.

56

Sunlight helps the body produce vitamin D, essential for building strong bones. It helps your brain, too, because a sunny day usually lifts spirits. Think how you feel when you look out in the morning and see the sun shining.

Although sunlight is good for your brain and health, too much sun can cause problems. As well as the danger of sunburn, there are risks of heatstroke or heat exhaustion from overheating. This can happen even if you're protected from direct sunshine. Overheating prevents your brain from working well and it can make you very ill.

So, do enjoy the benefits of sunny days by spending time outside, but be careful and tell an adult if you feel unwell.

WHAT IF YOU CAN'T DO SOME SORTS OF EXERCISE?

Many people have disabilities or illnesses that make some activities impossible, painful or difficult and it's vital to get good advice if that applies to you. But there are always fun, healthy things that you can do! The following pages have lots of ideas.

HOW TO USE THIS KNOWLEDGE

Maybe you love being active and you want to go outside and start giving your brilliant brain all the benefits NOW! Or maybe you're thinking, "Ugh, I hate this idea!"

I have suggestions for everyone. If you already like being active, you'll find more ideas here. If you don't think you like exercise, why not open your mind and find something to try? Be brave; be brilliant!

ACTIVITY IDEAS

Lots of these need only a ball and a space to play. Some cost money but most don't. Some you'll like and some you won't. Try as many as you can and you might be surprised. (Always follow appropriate safety rules.)

Things to do in a family or small group

- Play catch with ball or frisbee – try a "world championship" where you take the part of different countries

- French cricket
- Volleyball – buy a cheap net and ball
- A challenging walk – perhaps with a list of things to find
- An obstacle course in the garden or park

Things to do on your own or with one other person

- Go for a fast walk – time yourself over a route and see if you can beat it next time. (Always tell an adult where you're going.)
- Dance to music in your room
- Use a skipping-rope – see YouTube videos for tricks
- Practise a skill such as keepy-uppies or crossbar challenge
- Try a tennis trainer – a pole with a ball on a string
- Create a dance or gymnastics routine
- Create a routine of exercises, such as star jumps, squats, lunges and air punches

Things that could become hobbies

- Climbing on a climbing wall
- Tennis or badminton
- Gymnastics or dancing
- Any team sport
- Check your library or council website for local clubs

Things that are fun and exciting

- Visiting a waterpark or theme park
- Geocaching
- Organising a pretend "Olympics"
- A treasure hunt

Things that are peaceful and thoughtful

- Walking in a beautiful place
- Jogging
- Yoga or Pilates

Things that can work well with disabilities

🐾 Many sports have adapted versions – check local library or council website

🐾 If you use a wheelchair, exercising your upper body helps your heart and brain just like any other exercise – try playing catch or frisbee, or dancing with all the parts of your body that you can use

🐾 Using a punchbag or equipment for exercising arms

🐾 Exercise bands

🐾 Many of the ideas previously mentioned could also work for you, depending on your disability

BRILLIANT BRAIN BOOST

Moving your arms above the level of your heart means your heart has to work a bit harder. So, if you're having a five-minute exercise boost to push oxygen to your brain, increase the effect by lifting your arms up and down!

ACTIVITY FOR THIS CHAPTER

Make an activity chart for the next week. Add in the following information, including how long each will take:

- 👟 Any physical activities you'll be involved in at school
- 👟 Any physical activities you'll do outside school
- 👟 Any times you will walk at least part of the way to school or back home
- 👟 Any other things you'll walk to: shops, bus stop, a friend's house

Then, on any day when you don't have roughly an hour of activity, think what you could add in. Try to include a family activity or even something with a parent or sibling.

Pin this to your bedroom wall or somewhere where you'll see it. You could make a template and do this each week. And see if you can get other household members to do the same for themselves!

WHAT YOU'VE LEARNT

Activity and exercise boost your brain. More oxygen and glucose reach your brain (while also exercising your heart), your mood improves and you build fantastic physical and mental skills in all the areas where you want to excel. And while you're being physical, your brain is processing all your recent learning, as well as your experiences and emotions. You are becoming a healthier person with a more brilliant brain.

FOUR

SLEEP WELL

THE MAIN MESSAGE

Sleep is not a waste of time! It's vital to every aspect of health. It boosts your brain in lots of ways. In this chapter you'll learn how to get the best sleep possible and not to worry on nights when you can't.

WHAT YOU NEED TO KNOW

WHAT MAKES US SLEEP?

There are two things involved:

1. Sleep pressure – being awake makes you sleepy

From the moment you wake, your body starts to produce the chemical, adenosine, which builds up and makes you sleepy. This "sleep pressure" increases until you sleep.

2. Circadian rhythm – your body clock

You have a clock in your brain! Actually, you have two: one in each hemisphere. These clocks, although tiny, have a big name: the suprachiasmatic (SOOP-RA-KY-AS-MATIC) nucleus. Scientists sensibly just call this the SCN. Each SCN sits behind your eyes and is sensitive to daylight. It detects some daylight when your eyes are closed but more when they are open. The SCN's job is to judge the time of day. It does this mostly by noticing daylight or darkness. But it also uses other clues, such as daily routines, especially meals and winding down activities during the evening. If you have irregular mealtimes, no evening routine or look at bright light in the evening (including from screens), your SCN won't realise it's time for sleep.

When your SCN senses the approach of night-time, it prompts the hormone, melatonin, to prepare your body for sleep.

When your SCN detects morning, it reduces melatonin and you start to feel wakeful.

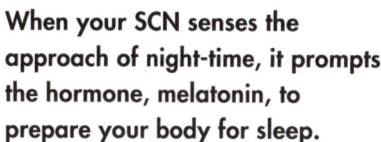

BRILLIANT BRAIN FACT

It's called circadian rhythm because in Latin "circa" means "about" and "dian" comes from the word for "day". Our circadian rhythm is roughly – but not exactly – a day long. It's on average 24 and a quarter hours long, with slight differences between ages. Teenagers and young adults have a longer "day" and much older adults a shorter one.

DOES EVERYONE HAVE THE SAME SIZE OF BRAIN?

People the same age have approximately the same size brain. Male brains are usually slightly bigger than female brains but only because male bodies are on average slightly bigger than female bodies. Having a bigger brain doesn't make a difference to how well it works.

HOW MUCH SLEEP DO WE NEED?

The figures scientists give for how much sleep we need are averages. You might not need the same as someone else your age. You'll know you're getting enough if you usually feel awake during the day.

Babies and young children need the most sleep, with the amount gradually decreasing as teenage years approach. But teenagers need a bit more, before arriving at adult sleep needs by the time they are in their mid twenties. In old age, many people need less than in middle age. Any time from eleven or twelve years old and until your early twenties, you develop teenage sleep patterns. Melatonin switches on later, so you won't feel sleepy until later at night. In the morning, it switches off later than for adults, so you might still feel sleepy when you get to school. You might want to sleep longer on weekend mornings.

On average, teenagers need around nine hours sleep. Many will feel fine if they get at least seven and a half, but some need more.

DIFFERENT SLEEP STAGES

The brain moves through different types or "stages" of sleep. Every night, we move through each stage several times.

Each stage is either called REM or NREM (non-REM). NREM is pronounced "en rem".

REM sleep

REM stands for Rapid Eye Movement, because your eyes flicker behind their lids. This is when dreaming happens. Although you can have very brief dream-like experiences in other sleep stages, the dreams you have during REM sleep have a sense of story, with things happening to you, often including strange things that couldn't really happen. When you explain them to someone the next day, they often don't make sense! More REM sleep happens at the end of the night, so if you wake too early you might miss some REM sleep.

NREM sleep

NREM sleep has three stages.

STAGE 1 (light NREM) – Very light sleep for two to five minutes. You can wake easily and will hardly feel you've been asleep.

STAGE 2 (light NREM) – Slightly deeper and more relaxed but still light sleep. It's a bit harder to wake but if you do you won't feel too groggy.

STAGE 3 (deep NREM) – It's very hard to be woken. If you do wake, you'll feel groggy. Most deep sleep is in the first half of the night.

HOW DOES SLEEP BUILD A BRILLIANT BRAIN?

Scientists are learning more and more as they study sleeping brains. But there's a lot we don't yet know. Perhaps you'll become a sleep scientist and discover new facts!

The sleep stages each bring different benefits but are equally important to the brain.

Emotional health

Dreams help people to process negative experiences. So, try not to worry about "bad dreams", as they're helping you. But if you have lots of really terrifying dreams, talk to a trusted adult. It's nothing to worry about but it's upsetting and talking helps.

Creativity and new ideas

While awake, we think logically and it can be difficult to let imagination fly free. But our dreaming mind lets us have surprising, new ideas.

LIGHT SLEEP BENEFITS

Learning new skills

If you practised a physical skill during the day – such as playing an instrument, learning a dance routine or sporting technique – your brain goes over the same actions during light sleep. You'll build and strengthen neural networks and clear up broken connections.

Creativity

Many people have used light sleep to improve their creativity. For example, inventor Thomas Edison would start an afternoon nap holding a metal ball above a saucer. As he drifted into sleep, the ball would drop onto the saucer with a crash and wake him. Then he'd jot down his new ideas.

BRILLIANT BRAIN FACT

During dreaming, your voluntary muscles (those you move by choice) are paralysed! Your heart and lungs work as normal but you can't deliberately move your body. This means you don't act out dreams.

DEEP SLEEP BENEFITS

Rest and restoration

Without enough deep sleep, you'll wake feeling unrefreshed. Deep sleep restores energy.

Growth and repair

Your brain releases hormones, including growth hormone. This doesn't only help you grow: it also repairs damaged cells.

Removing waste

Spaces open up between neurons, letting fluid wash away broken connections and dead cells.

Processing memories

New memories start in the hippocampus but in deep sleep they move into areas where long-term memories are formed, making space in the hippocampus for more new memories.

BRILLIANT BRAIN FACT

Dmitri Mendeleev was a Russian chemist who invented the periodic table, which lists all the chemical elements in a logical pattern. He discovered it in a dream! But he had to work at it: he'd been puzzling over it for ages. One day in February 1869, after yet another failure, he fell asleep and had a dream which suggested a solution. When he awoke, he realised that he'd solved the problem.

HOW TO USE THIS KNOWLEDGE

Everyone has a bad night's sleep sometimes. When you do, the pages that follow will help you. Even if you always sleep well, I bet you know someone who doesn't. If you share my advice, you can help them. The advice is the same for all ages!

HAVE A WINDING-DOWN PERIOD

A winding-down period before you turn your light off is essential. Anything between an hour and two hours is fine so I usually say one and a half hours.

First, work out what time you'll turn your light off. Here's how:

Decide how many hours you want to sleep – ideally around nine hours but eight will be fine.
Imagine you choose eight and a half

What time do you have to wake up?
Imagine that's 6.30 a.m.

So, what time should you fall asleep?
For eight and a half hours of sleep, that's 10 p.m.

But you won't fall asleep immediately so allow twenty minutes extra.
Light out at 9.40 p.m.

So, if you're turning your light off at 9.40 p.m., a winding-down time of one and a half hours would need to start at 8.10 p.m.

But what should you do in this time? The main thing is good "sleep hygiene". This is nothing to do with how clean you are! It's much more important.

HAVE GOOD SLEEP HYGIENE

Sleep hygiene is about making good choices during your winding-down time. Following these guidelines will help your brain and body become sleepy.

There are two elements:

1. Doing certain things (sleep positives) and avoiding others (sleep negatives)

2. Building a routine

Sleep positives

Include as many of these as you like during the one and a half hours before you want to sleep:

- Dark or dim light – close curtain/blind; switch off screens; use dim lamps
- Shower or bath
- Soft, slow music

- Lavender oil – a few drops in a bath or on a pillow
- Herbal sleep blend or balm, rubbed on your wrists and behind your ears
- Stretches or gentle yoga
- Light, unsugary snack, such as a small sandwich, cheese, fruit, cream cheese on oatcake, nuts
- Small milky drink or herbal tea
- Organising things for the morning and putting near door
- Folding clothes tidily
- Getting into sleeping clothes
- Cleaning face and brushing teeth
- Writing journal
- Drawing or colouring in
- Reading for pleasure
- Deep breathing exercise
- Moving slowly, calmly

Sleep negatives

Avoid all these during the winding-down period and earlier if possible:

- Daylight
- Bright electric light
- Screens apart from ebook readers
- Caffeine – in coffee, tea and cola drinks (unless "caffeine-free", herbal or fruit tea)
- Arguments and stress
- Exercise that raises heart rate
- Too much food; any spicy or rich food
- Work
- Loud, fast music
- Messy bedroom

Build a bedtime routine

Brains love a routine! If you do certain things in the same order each day, your brain quickly learns this and reacts to it. As soon as you start this routine, your brain recognises it as "what I do before sleep" and starts to get you ready to nod off.

How to do this:

1. Choose five to ten things from the sleep positives list and put them in whatever order will work for you. The only rule is that early on in the routine you should remove daylight from your room, by closing curtains and switching off screens.

2. Pin your list where it will remind you.

3. You'll need to do each thing at the same time and in the same order every evening. You'll notice the benefit after a few days.

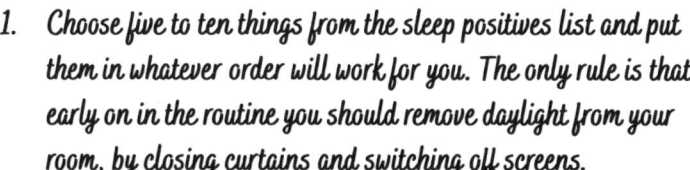

BRILLIANT BRAIN BOOST

If you're finding something difficult to grasp, think about it before sleep. Your sleeping brain might work it out. Sounds weird? It happens more often than you might think! (Remember the periodic table?) If you return to the problem the next day, you'll see an improvement. This means that failure is a step to success – but only if you don't give up! Be careful, though: worrying about something can keep you awake. So you need to make sure you're puzzling and thinking but not worrying!

AVOID SCREENS

You'll notice I mentioned screens in sleep negatives. There are two reasons why you should avoid them before bed:

1. Most screens emit light which is similar to daylight. When your brain thinks it's daytime it won't switch you into sleep mode.
2. Screens bring: messages that alert you; videos full of action and lights; and games to play.

Screens don't always harm sleep. Bedtime reading on an ebook reader can help you sleep, as long as you disable notifications and the screen is not too bright.

With phones, something that might help (though the science isn't clear) is the special night-time setting. But you still need to disable notifications and make sure your screen activity doesn't feel stressful. Using your phone or computer for anything interactive or social, including internet browsing or watching videos, is likely not to help. If you sleep well and get your eight to nine hours every night, that's fine. Otherwise, do your brain a favour and avoid screens before bed.

WHAT TO DO WHEN YOU CAN'T SLEEP

Everyone experiences this sometimes and it's not pleasant.
Here are my tips:

- Don't worry about tomorrow. If you have a test or performance, your body will produce adrenalin, keeping your brain alert and brilliant.

- Don't look at your clock. Knowing the time increases anxiety.

- Don't think about falling asleep. It's often best not to try too hard.

- Let your muscles soften and relax. Sink your shoulders; think about each muscle and focus on making it soft, heavy and relaxed.

- Slow your breathing, focusing on your breaths. Perhaps count them.

- Let your mind relax. Imagine your brain being stroked by soft fingers.

- Focus your mind on something positive (or boring) so it doesn't return to your worries. (Try the ideas on the next page.)

- Don't lie there too long. If you feel you've been trying for longer than about twenty minutes and you're nowhere near sleep, get up and do something gentle and relaxing. Don't switch a screen or bright lights on; maybe read or do a jigsaw.

WHAT TO THINK ABOUT WHEN YOU CAN'T SLEEP

Everything seems worse at night and it can be hard to stop negative thoughts. Or your brain might be alert and excited. Whichever happens to you, try these ideas to calm your mind:

Imagine a place you'd love to be. A soft sandy beach? The warm grass of a local park? In your garden eating strawberries? On the moon? Build up detail. You can add people or pets or be on your own.

Be the hero in an imaginary adventure. Again, build details, people, actions, excitement.

BRILLIANT BRAIN FACT

You dream several times every night but you'll only be aware of that if you wake up in the middle of a dream. Sometimes, if you go straight back to sleep you can return to the same dream. So, if you have a bad dream and don't want to return to it, make sure you wake up properly and shift position before going back to sleep.

Play a word game. For each letter of the alphabet, name an animal, sporting hero, cartoon character, person from history or in your school.

Count slowly backwards from 100.

Count sheep. Picture lots of them jumping a ditch one by one: they keep trying to confuse you, by hiding or going in threes or going in the wrong direction.

How would you spend a lottery win? Or any daydream you like. "If I could be anything..." "My ideal life..." "I would be proudest if..."

ACTIVITY FOR THIS CHAPTER

Design a poster with your winding-down routine. It can be pictures or words or both. Feel relaxed and think about sleep as you're doing it. Pin it to your door or by your bed. This helps fix the ideas in your mind.

WHAT YOU'VE LEARNT

Sleep is more important than people used to think. Most people your age need on average eight to nine hours to let their brain do its best job. Sleep helps restore energy and repair cells but it's also vital for learning, mental health, memory and creativity. Now you know how to get the best sleep possible: lots of sleep positives, avoid sleep negatives, build a winding-down routine and train yourself to focus on relaxing or boring thoughts rather than worries and stresses.

FIVE

MAKE FRIENDS

THE MAIN MESSAGE

Humans are wired to make connections with other people but sometimes friendships are difficult. This chapter looks at why friends and supporters are important for your brain and how to build good bonds with the right people.

WHAT YOU NEED TO KNOW

YOUR BRAIN IS WIRED TO BE SOCIAL

Remember that your brain is wired just like the brains of our earliest ancestors. Early humans would have been safer in groups than alone. They would be likely to live longer and more healthily if they worked together. They could collaborate to build houses, make tools, collect firewood, hunt and gather food. They could look after each other if sick or injured. If a parent was ill, someone else would look after the children.

The same applies to humans today. Think of things we can only do because we work together and share knowledge: designing and building technology, machines, hospitals, vehicles and every piece of equipment we use daily. Some people love to work on their own. But they benefit from knowledge from others. Even individuals who like being on their own need other people.

Brains are wired to be social because living, working and communicating with others gives people better chances of survival and success. Your brain needs other brains!

82

Human society is like an enormous network of brains and yours is part of it.

WHAT HAPPENS IN YOUR BRAIN TO MAKE YOU SOCIAL?

There are two chemicals involved:

Dopamine

The brain encourages us to do things by giving us a burst of pleasure. In your brain's reward system, you get a buzz of dopamine, the brain chemical that makes you feel excited and positive, when you have an opportunity to do something your brain is wired for – like being social. So, at any chance to be social, dopamine gives you a push to inspire you to do it.

Oxytocin

Oxytocin, the "love hormone", is produced when we feel any affection or positive feeling for someone. This might be a strong feeling, such as when someone falls in love or when a mother looks at or hears her baby. Or it could be a smaller feeling, such as when someone we like gives us a hug or we see a friend in a room of strangers. The positive feeling from oxytocin encourages us to be social by making us enjoy being with people we like.

ARE TEENAGE BRAINS DIFFERENT?

People of all ages need human contact. But social behaviour is particularly important for adolescents: what people think of you; whether you fit into that group or another group or no group; being accepted; blending in or standing out – these matter a lot.

Two aspects of teenage life help explain this:

1. Becoming independent

Adolescence is a biological stage moving you away from adult protection so that one day you'll be independent. It becomes more important to bond with your peers. That might mean doing what your friends want rather than what adults want. Peer pressure is extremely powerful.

2. Surrounded by people

If you're at school you're surrounded by people. And if you're on social media you'll probably have contacts you've never met but who are still part of your network. Although humans are social, maintaining friendships takes time and energy and it is not possible to manage too many. That pressure can feel huge.

HOW DOES YOUR BRAIN INFLUENCE YOUR FEELINGS?

Your brain creates your feelings. It takes in information (such as things you see and hear), processes it with your memories and personality and whatever is happening to you at the time, and creates the feelings that you notice.

QUESTION FROM YOU

GRACE ASKED

INTROVERTS AND EXTROVERTS

Some people feel a strong need for time on their own (even if they also sometimes enjoy social activity). They often prefer quiet activities with one or two friends, rather than lively parties. They become tired and even stressed when with others too much. These people are more "introverted".

Some people don't need much time alone and might not enjoy being alone. They like activities which are loud and exciting and involve lots of people. They feel energised when with others. These people are more "extroverted".

Some people are a complete mixture and some change depending on the situation or how they feel.

Both introverts and extroverts need friends. But they have different preferences for how to spend time with their friends. And if they don't get the right type of social time they can feel anxious, unhappy or stressed.

Introverts and extroverts are equally valuable! But extroverts' brains are wired in ways that make it easier for them to be social and also to work in a team. Introverts have to work harder to let their social skills flourish.

You'll find tips for introverts and extroverts on page 90.

HOW YOUR SOCIAL BRAIN CAN CAUSE PROBLEMS

When we build a friendship or connection we often share information about ourselves. Usually, there's no problem. Sharing things about your life and likes is part of getting to know someone.

But some things you might share and later regret. For example:

- ☑ Where you live
- ☑ A negative opinion of someone
- ☑ A secret
- ☑ A revealing or embarrassing photo of yourself
- ☑ A revealing or embarrassing photo of someone else

Any of these could cause a big problem. Those last two things could, in fact, be illegal: if the person in the photo is below a legal age and is shown naked or in an inappropriate or sexual way.

So we all need to be aware that our wonderfully social brain can get us into trouble if we aren't careful. See page 98 for practical ways to use this information.

WHAT HAPPENS TO YOUR BRAIN IF YOU AREN'T SOCIAL?

Because our brains are wired to be social, there can be problems if we avoid social activity too much. Your reasons for avoiding social activity might be because you're happy alone or because you're anxious about it or because you've had a bad experience. Whatever the reason, you need to exercise your social brain. But what happens if you don't?

If you can't make friends, you can feel lonely. That's a horrible feeling. Loneliness puts people at risk of mental health problems such as depression.

Making friends takes practice, so if you are never social then you might find it difficult if you want to make friends later.

Even if you like being alone, your brain will benefit from making connections with other people. You can have fun, share good or bad news, learn new things, find interesting opportunities and build brilliant brains together.

HOW TO USE THIS KNOWLEDGE

Now that you know why spending time with other people is important for your brain, here's how you can get the benefits!

KNOW YOUR TEAM

Think about people you feel positive about. People you like seeing or who make you feel happy if they smile at you or greet you by name. Think of:

People who live with you
Friends at school
Friends who live nearby
Friends who live far away
Relatives who don't live with you
Adults who work at your school or youth group or elsewhere
People from other schools or homes you've had
Any other adults who make you feel positive
Any other young people who make you feel positive

Write them down. They are your team. They could be there for you any time you need. You'll choose different ones for different situations but they're all there. You can call on them and they'll be there for you.

Pick five people from your team and remember a time when they made you feel happy, positive or good in some way. Which ones would you talk to if you felt down? Or if you needed help or advice? Or if you wanted to share something exciting?

KNOW YOURSELF

Although all humans share lots of feelings and behaviours, people are also all individual, with different likes and dislikes. Knowing your own personality will help you choose suitable activities for your brain. See what you can identify in the following pages so that you can make choices that work for you.

Introvert?

Look at page 85 if you need to remind yourself about these two personalities.

If you're more introverted, make sure you get enough time alone but don't isolate yourself. Sometimes, you need to go out with friends when you don't feel like it. Have some quiet time afterwards, if you need that. Understand that some people are naturally livelier and more excitable than others: they are not better or worse than you, just different.

Here are some tips for introverts to build their social skills:

1.
Don't worry how many friends you have: the number is not important. You need quality: just a few people you trust and like being with.

2.
You might find it easier to be good friends with someone who has the same likes as you: for example, another quiet and thoughtful person rather than a very lively and noisy person. If you do have a noisy friend, that's great but it's OK to tell them that you need to be on your own sometimes!

3.
When someone asks you to a party or to join an activity, try to say yes. If you're anxious (like many people), team up with someone else and arrange to go together.

4.
If you find it hard to start a conversation, think of a topic or question in advance. Asking a question can be a simple way to start a chat.

5.
When you're with other people, it doesn't matter if you're quiet and don't know what to say. Just smile and laugh with everyone else and they will like the fact you're there and you're listening.

6.
Chatting online or via text can be a good way to get to know someone. You can take time to work out the right words.

7.
As with anything you want your brain to do, practice is essential. So, though I want you to value your introvert side, I urge you to boost your extrovert skills by taking social opportunities when you see them. It will get easier, I promise!

Extrovert?

If you're more of an extrovert, notice what activities make you happy and look out for opportunities to do them each weekend. But practise amusing yourself sometimes, too. Don't take offence if friends don't always want to come out. When someone wants to do a quiet activity, that doesn't mean they're boring: everyone enjoys different things!

Shy?

Do you think you're a shy person and very self-conscious when you feel people are looking at you? Don't be hard on yourself. Feeling shy is so natural and especially common for young people. With help, you can learn to deal with it.

You can overcome shyness with practice and small steps. Maybe buddy up with someone you trust and support each other through small challenges such as speaking to a shop assistant, making a short phone call, or asking your friend's parent a question. The more you do this, the easier it will get.

Highly sensitive?

Being sensitive is good: it means you think about other people. But being too sensitive can cause problems: you might be hurt; you might waste time worrying about things you can't change; and you might always put other people first instead of valuing yourself.

Be your own best friend. Think what a kind friend would say to you and say it to yourself. For example, a friend might say "Don't worry – you're a good person." So, say that to yourself.

Insecure?

Insecurity means feeling negative about yourself, thinking you aren't good enough or that others don't like you. Even confident-seeming people sometimes feel this. Being insecure can cause problems in a friendship: you might focus too much on what you think is wrong with you; you might feel or act jealous; you might constantly ask for reassurance, which can be annoying.

Notice when you (or your friend) say or do something because of self-doubt. Grow friendships where both of you give praise and reassurance.

In general, try to learn what makes you feel and work well and what makes you feel and work badly. This doesn't mean being selfish or only thinking of yourself but it does mean being your own first supporter. Then you can be better at helping others.

WORK AT YOUR FRIENDSHIPS

Now you know who's on your team, how can you make those friendships and connections even stronger? You'll be able to do these things whatever type of person you are!

- ☑ **Keep in touch** – Not every day but if you ignore someone for too long the bond can weaken. Let them know you're there; ask how they are; send a message.

- ☑ **Mark their special days** – Birthdays; successes; things they've been worried or excited about. Show them you remembered.

- ☑ **Support their distress** – If you know they're upset, scared, anxious, show you're thinking of them, even if you can't solve the problem.

- ✉ **Listen** – When someone says something they're worried about, try not to dismiss it; listen and say you're sorry they feel like that.

- ✉ **Give little things** – A card, smile, tiny present, message. Don't embarrass by doing too much, especially where money is involved. If they couldn't do the same for you it might make them uncomfortable. It's often best to spend no money.

- ✉ **Notice who's left out** – Sometimes quiet people get left out because others forget they're there. If that's happening to someone you know, is there a way you can make sure they're included if they want to be?

BRILLIANT BRAIN FACT

Research shows that we laugh much more with other people than on our own and that friends laugh together more than strangers do. And laughter is good for us. So if you're feeling down, doing something with friends could give you lots of chances for that much-needed laugh.

MAKE NEW CONTACTS

Your life will have various friendships. Some will be meaningful and deep, maybe lasting years. Others will be less important and shorter. You don't know at the beginning which will be which but if you don't make new connections they won't exist at all!

Here are some things to try:

- ☑ Is there someone in your year group you've never spoken to? Try speaking to them tomorrow.

- ☑ Is there a party or activity coming up where you're going to meet new people? Plan what you'll say to someone for the first time.

- ☑ Are you in an online group? Think of a question you could ask to show an interest in someone.

- ☑ Remember that friendships start with sharing information. Write down three things you'd be happy for people to know about you.

USE SOCIAL MEDIA WELL

Social media includes all the ways that technology and our devices allow us to connect with others. Here are some ways it can help your social brain:

- ☒ If you're quite shy, you can get to know people easily.

- ☒ If there's a group conversation, you can be heard.

- ☒ You can have conversations with people in other time zones.

- ☒ You can have more than one chat at once.

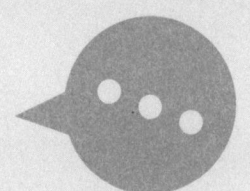

- ☒ If you feel different from those around you, you can find similar people online.

- ☒ If you feel anxious or upset, you can talk to a friend even if they aren't with you.

- ☒ You can think carefully about what to say in advance, which can be useful if it's a tricky subject.

But social media can also cause problems. Here's how to recognise these and avoid them:

- Spending a long time on social media means less time to build other skills, so it makes a difference to how your brain is wired.

  Make plenty of time for exercise, face-to-face chat, other hobbies, schoolwork and family.

- It's easy to send a message you may regret, especially when angry or upset. In normal conversation you can just say sorry, but a written message often stays and can be shared.

  Think before you click. Look ahead to how you might feel later. Never send messages when angry or upset.

- You might send a photo or video you regret. It can be difficult or impossible to take it back. (And might be illegal to send.)

  Think whether you'd be happy for your parents and grandparents to see what you're sending. If not, don't!

☑ The person you're communicating with might not be who they say they are. They could be dangerous.

Never give personal details (address, school, full name, parents' names or jobs, even a pet's name) and never agree to meet someone you haven't met before. If someone asks to meet you or wants personal details, tell a trusted adult. If you feel uncomfortable, tell someone.

☑ People who are shy might use social media to avoid real-life contact, but face-to-face conversation is important.

Practise face-to-face skills: the more you do it the easier it will become. It's a good idea to start with someone you feel comfortable with.

☑ Using social media in the hour or two before bed can prevent sleep – see Chapter Four.

Switch off all mobile and internet-enabled devices up to two hours before bedtime.

ACTIVITY FOR THIS CHAPTER

Think of one or two people you are friends with or who you feel positive about. They can be your age or adults. Write down their names or draw a picture of them, and below this write the following:

Three good things about them.

A time they helped you or did something that made you feel good.

A time you helped them or tried to make them feel good.

What kind of problem they could help you with.

What kind of things you enjoy doing with them.

Describe the first time you met or spoke to them.

What you will say to them next time you see them.

WHAT YOU'VE LEARNT

Everyone needs their support network. It doesn't have to be a big group but you need to know who they are and that they're there. Some people like big, noisy social interaction while others prefer smaller, quieter groups or one-to-one conversations. Face-to-face conversation can be harder than online but it's important and rewarding so you need to practise: it will get easier and more fun.

SIX

BOUNCE BACK

THE MAIN MESSAGE

No one likes bad things happening
to them. Everyone needs strength
to bounce back and find confidence
after a setback, whether big or
small. This ability to bounce back is
often called resilience. And resilience,
like all skills, begins in the brain.

WHAT YOU NEED TO KNOW

WHAT EXACTLY IS RESILIENCE?

How well do you pick yourself up after a bad thing has happened? "Bad things" can be anything from minor disappointments to major disasters. It can be hard to recover after a setback, to find the confidence to keep going and grasp new opportunities. This ability to bounce back is resilience.

You won't bounce back exactly the same as you were before. Every experience makes new memories and those memories become a new part of you. You might be stronger!

You also don't have to bounce back from a bad time immediately. It's natural to feel overwhelmed for a while. It's OK to cry or need help. Even very bouncy people sometimes don't feel bouncy.

Being resilient means you can look back and say:

I dealt with that. Now I can learn from it. If it happens again, my experience will help me manage it better.

Resilience lets us learn from mistakes and have a better chance of success next time.

ARE SOME PEOPLE JUST MORE RESILIENT?

It sometimes looks that way. You might have a friend who seems to sail through tough times and doesn't seem bothered by failing a test, or anxious about the future. Are they naturally bouncier and stronger? Not necessarily. Here are other reasons why some people seem more resilient:

◎ They might have lots of support.

◎ Perhaps their early life was secure and smooth. When difficult things happen to young children, they can find it harder to grow resilience.

◎ They might not be very bothered about failure.

◎ They might have a growth mindset, rather than a fixed one.

◎ They might be good at hiding feelings but still be distressed inside.

Some people have an easier time but everyone can become more resilient. Resilience is a skill and that means we can improve it, if we choose to learn how.

DO BAD THINGS ALWAYS MAKE US STRONGER?

Not always. Sometimes we don't get the help we need to cope. Sometimes it's just too difficult. If you feel that something has knocked you down and you haven't bounced back, I have two messages.

Don't blame yourself. Even adults find things tough sometimes.

The time you didn't bounce back is the past, not the future. From now on, you can learn to become resilient and be confident. You can grow a bouncy brain!

BRILLIANT BRAIN BOOST

Think of someone who has helped you in the last few months. Maybe someone said a kind thing or listened to a problem. Perhaps someone made you feel good about yourself. Maybe someone stood up for you when you needed it.

Can you tell them you are grateful? Could you write a thank you message to an adult who has helped or supported you?

WHAT PART OF THE BRAIN CAUSES PEOPLE TO SUFFER ANXIETY?

The amygdala triggers the stress response when it senses a threat. The threat could be a worrying thought, so even if you just think of something you're nervous about your amygdala triggers anxiety.

WHAT HAS RESILIENCE GOT TO DO WITH THE BRAIN?

There are two reasons why resilience is relevant in a book about building a brilliant brain. First, resilience is a set of mental skills and it takes place in the brain. It is about how you feel, think and behave. Your brain is where you think and feel and is the place where behaviours start.

And secondly, being resilient helps your brain learn other things. This is because resilience gives you confidence, the desire to learn and the belief that you can learn from mistakes. If bad things in life knock you down all the time and you find it too hard to pick yourself up and keep on trying, you'll miss so many opportunities for learning, thriving and having the best life possible.

Let's look at how you can improve your resilience and so build a better brain.

HOW TO USE THIS KNOWLEDGE

Here are some things to think about to prepare for the next time you are dealing with a setback.

REMEMBER GROWTH MINDSET

In Chapter One you learnt about growth mindset:

"I can become better at any skill by learning and practising and keeping on trying."

You might want to go back and look at that chapter again to remind yourself how important it is.

Growth mindset is connected to resilience because it reassures you that you can improve skills by practising them. And, since resilience is a skill, you can build resilience by trying, practising and watching other people behave and talk in resilient ways.

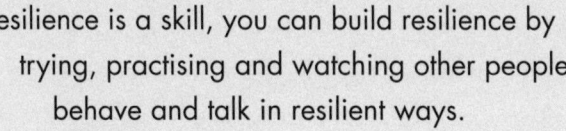

DEAL WITH FAILURE

No one likes to fail. I certainly don't! But the only people who never fail are those who only try easy things. They don't risk failure but they don't get the satisfaction of succeeding at something challenging.

Things we call failure can be small or big. Small things might be getting a question wrong in class or not doing a piece of work well. Some people will care more than others. Big things might be failing an important test or not winning a competition you worked hard for.

Failure could involve messing up and being criticised. That can be very upsetting. You might feel you let yourself or someone else down.

A failure could be caused mostly by bad luck: perhaps you had a cold the day of your audition. Or you slipped when you started your race.

Failure can also happen because someone else was better: maybe your gymnastics rival pulled out a performance that you simply couldn't beat.

And failure can be either wholly or partly your fault. Maybe you didn't listen or work hard enough. Maybe you didn't eat breakfast.

Failure can be very personal, with no one else noticing. Or it can be more public. You might feel that people are judging or laughing at you, even though it's none of their business.

However you believe you've failed, here's what to do:

First, allow yourself to feel upset, annoyed or embarrassed if you want to, but only for the shortest possible time.

Next, work out why it happened. How much was luck and how much was something you could have done differently?

Now forget about the luck elements: focus on the things you could do differently.

You are now being resilient! If you can use the same ideas next time you need them, I'd call that being super-resilient!

BRILLIANT BRAIN BOOST

I think "failure" sounds too final. I prefer to call it a stumble. When you fall, you don't stay on the ground: you pick yourself up. You see what tripped you. If you weren't paying attention, you decide to be more careful next time. If you couldn't have avoided it, you move on.

TIPS FOR PERFECTIONISTS

Some people need to get everything right and always be the best. People like that are called perfectionists and they have two problems:

> They forget to be proud of what they've achieved.

> They feel so bad when they mess up that they can't stop thinking about it. Then they miss the chance to improve.

It's good to be ambitious but people can't be perfect all the time. If that sounds like you, try these tips when you make mistakes:

Recognise the good things about being a perfectionist: you'll aim high and will often do well. But appreciate that this can make you feel worse when things go wrong.

When you think everyone's laughing at you, know that they're not. And if they are, what a waste of time! It's not making their own lives or brains better.

Remind yourself that although it feels bad when something goes wrong, soon you'll feel differently.

Remember growth mindset: the way to do better is to keep trying.

Be a good friend to yourself: what would you say to a friend in this situation?

Share your feelings with someone you trust. Talking and listening really help.

KEEP THE RIGHT PEOPLE AROUND YOU

The people you spend time with will affect you in many ways: not just your thoughts but also behaviours and emotions. When those people are happy and excited, you probably will be, too. When they're sad or stressed, that pulls your mood down.

If people around you show resilience, courage and calmness, that will help you grow those strengths, too.

So, when possible, it's helpful to spend time with people who are good role models for resilience.

But it's not always possible. Suppose someone close to you is going through a tough time and feeling overwhelmed. Suppose they're finding it hard to be resilient and stay positive. You don't want to desert them so what can you do to stay strong yourself while also supporting them? Here is some advice:

◎ Make sure you also spend time with people whose mood is positive and who make you feel positive.

◎ Make sure you spend time looking after your health, by eating well, sleeping enough, having plenty of physical activity and taking breaks. If you don't look after yourself, you can't help others.

◎ If you can, encourage them to get support from an adult who can help. You should not have to take their problems on your shoulders.

◎ Get them to read this book. It has advice for all ages!

TRUST YOUR SUPPORT NETWORK

Being resilient doesn't mean you have to deal with everything on your own. Humans are successful because they help each other.

Who might help you if you asked? Look back at the Know Your Team section on page 89 to remind yourself of who's on your side, and try the activity on page 100.

Different people can help in different situations. You can choose who to go to with any problem or worry.

When you feel confident that you have people who are on your side, you will automatically be more resilient than you were. You will be stronger in the face of any problems because you know someone is there to help if you need it.

BRILLIANT BRAIN BOOST

Think of a good deed you could do for anyone you know. Doing a kind act for someone else has several good results: it helps the other person; it builds a bond between you and them; it makes you feel good about yourself, giving you a brain boost; and it makes the world better!

USE GREAT COPING STRATEGIES

When life is difficult, we need healthy, useful actions to keep us strong. These actions are called positive coping strategies. Here are some great suggestions for you to choose from.

Talk to someone

Most people love to be asked for help. It shows you trust that person.

Another person might not have an answer but that doesn't matter. The important part is sharing the worry or emotion. Often at stressful times our thoughts feel muddled, overwhelming or dark. Just talking to someone else is a positive coping strategy.

If your appetite is affected, this is normal and it won't do any harm for a short while. But as soon as possible, get yourself on track with the good choices you learnt about in Chapter Two.

Make sure you get enough sleep. If anxiety is making that difficult, check out the tips in Chapter Four.

Look after your physical health

When people go through tough times, they often forget to look after themselves. Even if you don't feel like going for a walk or a swim or having a kick about with your friends in the park, it will really help you feel better. Chapter Three has everything about that.

If you like reading, make sure you have an engaging book to escape into when you get into bed. Or listen to relaxing music or an audio book. See Chapter Nine for more about the power of reading.

Be your own best friend

If a friend was going through this, what would you say to them? How would you reassure and support them? Or how would you take their mind off worries? Be that voice for yourself!

Be grateful for something

Whatever you're going through, there will also be something to be glad about and grateful for. You might be glad that it's a sunny day, that you have good friends, that your dad cooked your favourite meal. You can even think about how things could be worse and you're glad they're not.

You might need help finding something to be glad about, but talking to someone else will give you ideas.

Give yourself praise

You are dealing with a bad thing. It's not going to crush you. You are going to get through it and even learn how to be a better, stronger, kinder human being.

WELL DONE, YOU!

KEEP A JOURNAL

Lots of people find writing a journal really useful and uplifting. You don't have to be great at writing, though you'll get better – and now you know why! You can use a notebook or computer and it's not for anyone else to look at so the spelling and style don't matter. You can draw, if you want to, or use emojis to record your feelings. You don't have to write your journal every day, but lots of people find it's a great habit to get into.

You could get a ready-made journal, which has prompts and sections to fill in so you don't have to think too much. Some of these journals have tips or ask questions to help you decide what to write. And having boxes to fill instead of a blank page can make it quicker and easier.

Why journalling can be useful

Many people find it healing to write about things that happen to them – bad and good – and to express feelings and thoughts in writing. It is a bit like sharing your problems by talking to someone, except that you're not talking to a real person. Some people find it easier than talking. But others find it unhelpful and even upsetting, so follow your instinct – if it's not helping, don't do it!

ACTIVITY FOR THIS CHAPTER

Think of a bad experience you remember. It should be from at least several months ago. In your notebook, write down:

1. The main emotions you felt at the time.

2. On a scale of one to ten, how bad did you feel at the time? Can you remember any thoughts you had?

3. On a scale of one to ten, how bad do you feel about it right now? Have the thoughts you had changed?

4. How do you think the experience changed you in a positive way? Perhaps, "It has helped me understand how others feel" or "It taught me how to help someone else who might go through the same thing" or "It showed me that I am stronger than I thought" or "I thought I couldn't cope but I did".

5. Is there something you would do differently if this happened again?

You just showed your resilience skills!

WHAT YOU'VE LEARNT

You've started to make your brain – and yourself – more resilient. You've learnt that the ability to bounce back from a setback or disaster is something you can grow. You know you don't need to beat yourself up when you feel overwhelmed because even adults struggle sometimes. You have a growth mindset, not a fixed one. You know bad things happen but you can deal with them if you keep trying and you can ask for help when you need. You have learnt good coping strategies for bad times and you've grown the confidence to keep trying. You've learnt to be more resilient!

SEVEN

BE CURIOUS

THE MAIN MESSAGE

Humans are wired to be curious because learning brings advantages. But curiosity can get us into trouble or danger. And it can be distracting if we're trying to concentrate. So, we need to be curious but we need to do it thoughtfully.

WHAT YOU NEED TO KNOW

YOU ARE WIRED TO BE CURIOUS

Think about early humans: if they weren't curious, they never would have discovered new things. They wouldn't have:

Tried new foods
Explored new places
Designed tools or wheels or shelters
Invented interesting ways to solve problems
Asked themselves, "I wonder what would happen if I did that?"

Humans are still wired to be curious today. Without that curiosity there wouldn't be electricity, medicines, aeroplanes, books, computers, phones, games or any other gadgets.

You can see this curiosity in babies. They pick everything up, especially things they haven't seen before. If babies waited for everything to be handed to them, they would learn about the world much more slowly. If you wait for people to tell you everything, you will learn things slowly, too.

Being curious is about wanting to find out, wanting to explore and discover. Being curious helps your brain develop fast.

BRAINS LIKE NOVELTY

There are two quite opposite things that your brain naturally likes:

FAMILIARITY

Things you've experienced before.
For example, when you're choosing food
in a school canteen or an item in a shop,
your eyes are drawn to what you know and
like. You see those more easily.

NOVELTY

Things that are new, different, surprising. These
wake your brain up. For example, a giraffe in a
herd of horses would alert your brain more than a
giraffe in a herd of giraffes. Visiting somewhere
you've never been before, hearing different
music, tasting a new food, meeting
a new person: these make you
pay attention.

Novelty wakes your brain so it can learn important new things.
Familiarity means you don't need to spend much brain energy on
routine decisions, leaving attention for new things.

BRILLIANT BRAIN BOOST

Ask questions! When you don't understand something, either ask
a person or use a book or the internet. Asking questions is a sign
of intelligence and the way to become cleverer and wiser.

CURIOSITY CAN SPOIL CONCENTRATION

Do you have a mobile phone? Or another device that sends you notifications? Do you use social media? If you answered yes to any of those questions, ask yourself:

When you're trying to concentrate on work, does your phone or social media keep distracting you?

Do you sometimes spend longer on your devices than you mean to because you keep finding more to look at?

That's your natural curiosity harming your concentration. You are trying to "multitask". The truth about multitasking is this: if a task needs concentration, you will not do it so well if other things occupy your attention. That's the same for everyone, whatever age.

For example, if you are trying to do homework or read a book, you cannot do it properly if:

- You're watching or listening to television or a video.
- Someone is talking to you.
- Messages or notifications arrive.
- Adverts or moving images come onto your screen.
- You keep thinking about something else.

Listening to music can be OK because it uses almost no concentration and it can help you ignore distractions.

We concentrate better when we try to focus on one thing. Sometimes we need not to be quite so curious! That's what I mean by being curious but also thoughtful and sensible.

BRILLIANT BRAIN FACT

When neurons are active, they produce a tiny amount of electricity. If all your neurons were active at the same time (which they wouldn't be) you'd produce enough electricity to power a lightbulb. In 2015, science journalist Maddie Stone showed that you could (in theory) charge a smartphone in around 70 hours using the power from your brain. Unfortunately, you'd have no brain energy left for anything else, including breathing. And there isn't a way to harness the elecricity, so it would be impossible anyway!

CURIOSITY CAN BE RISKY

Imagine a baby being curious about an electric socket. The baby is trying to learn about the world but in this situation curiosity can be dangerous. You are better than a baby at staying safe while still being curious.

Imagine that you aren't sure whether something is risky. You can:

Use your experience to guess and to check if necessary.

Ask a trusted adult and if they don't know, they can ask someone else.

Ask friends and if they don't know, they can ask someone else.

Get information from a book or the internet.

Humans are wired to be afraid of things, too, because that helps keep curiosity at the right level. You need the right amount of fear and curiosity! You need to be brave but not foolish.

QUESTION FROM YOU

DOES YOUR BRAIN GROW WITH YOU?

Yes and no. It doubles in size during your first year of life but reaches full size between the ages of eleven and fourteen, on average. Your body will carry on growing for longer than your brain does.

EVIE ASKED

HOW TO USE THIS KNOWLEDGE

Here are some ideas for how to harness curiosity to build your brilliant brain.

PRACTISE UNI-TASKING

When we try to multitask, we don't do so well. So, when you have a task that needs concentration, practise "uni-tasking", doing one thing at a time. Here's how:

- Make sure your phone is out of sight and switched off. Ideally in another room.

- If you need a computer or device for the task, close apps and windows that you're not using, including the internet, if possible.

- Set a timer for how long you want to focus for. Tell people not to disturb you for this period.

- If your mind wanders, pull your focus back to the task and say, "I am concentrating well now."

- If listening to music helps you concentrate, that's fine. Music can help prevent distractions, but choose familiar music and don't play it too loudly.

USE ALL PARTS OF YOUR BRAIN

If you spend too much time on one type of learning, other brain areas will miss out. Here are activities which use different brain areas. Choose the biggest variety you can to exercise your curiosity and desire to learn.

A physical activity using fingers –
such as playing an instrument, using a keyboard or drawing

Social activities with people in the same room

Reading for pleasure

Writing – imaginative, opinion, letters, poetry, explanation, information

Art and craft – drawing, painting, clothes designing, constructing

Inventing and problem-solving

Discussing ideas – persuading, disagreeing, understanding

Daydreaming, imagining, thinking, meditating

Experiencing music – appreciating, playing, listening, remembering, copying, singing

Finding your way – reading maps, learning routes

Being observant – looking, smelling, tasting, listening

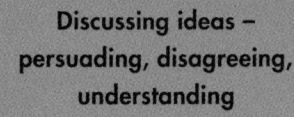

BRILLIANT BRAIN BOOST

Which of these have you done in the last week? Give yourself a point for each one. See if next week you can do even better.

Which of these do you rarely or never do? Aim to find a way to bring those brilliant activities into your life. Maybe get together with a friend and work out how you could do that, so your brain has the chance to try different things and use its natural curiosity.

MAKE IT INTERESTING

Learning is easier when we are interested in our work. It's more enjoyable and effective. But what if you have to learn something you find boring? How can you make yourself curious? Here are some ideas:

Study it in a place that makes you happy. Sit on the grass with a refreshing drink or curl up in front of a fire.

Make it look different. Write your notes in sparkly pen or a crazy font.

Read it in a funny voice.

Learn it while walking. Or standing on one leg.

Give yourself a challenging time limit. Set an alarm and tell yourself what you must do in that time; praise yourself if you succeed or make a good attempt.

Promise yourself a rewarding break afterwards.

Break it into smaller chunks and alternate these with fun things.

How would your favourite teacher make it interesting? Song and dance? Game?

Collaborate with a friend.

BECOME AN EXPERT

You can become an expert in anything that interests you! Some expertise is about facts. You could be an expert on the history of your country or the life of a famous person.

Other expertise involves improving a skill. You could become an expert baker, piano player, footballer or coder. Some skills also need knowledge: for example, with coding, you learn the rules and language as well as practising doing it.

Feeling good about your achievements makes you more likely to be curious again! Here are some things you could become expert in:

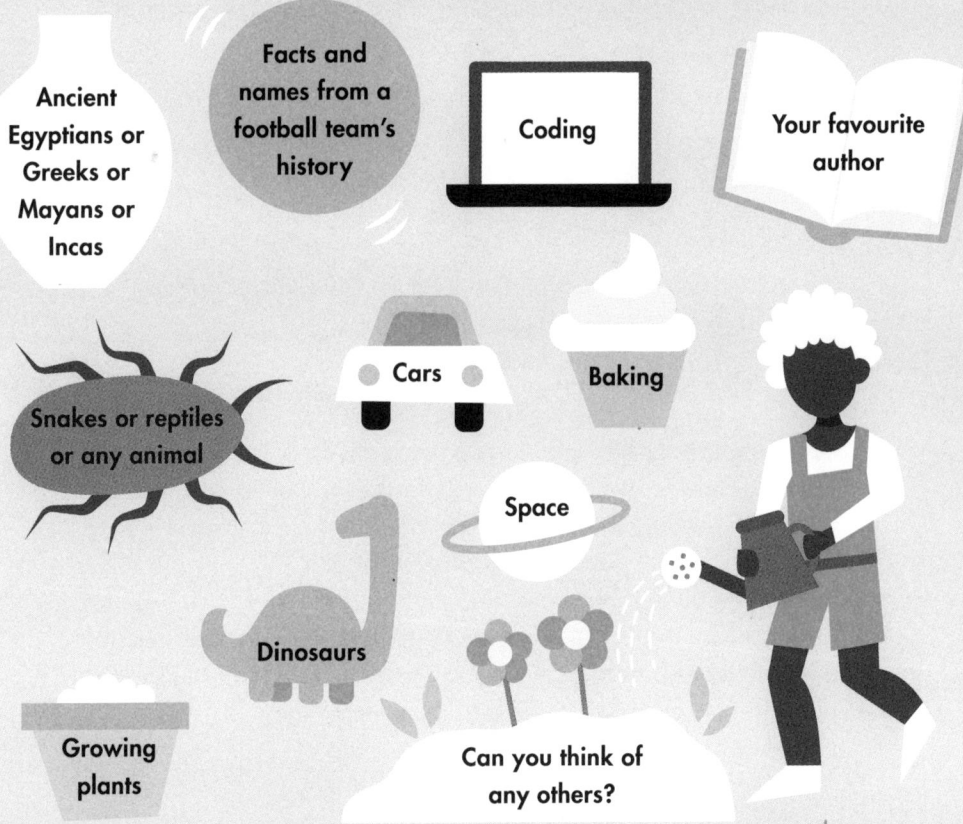

Ancient Egyptians or Greeks or Mayans or Incas

Facts and names from a football team's history

Coding

Your favourite author

Snakes or reptiles or any animal

Cars

Baking

Space

Dinosaurs

Growing plants

Can you think of any others?

ACTIVITY FOR THIS CHAPTER

Make a quiz for family or friends. Find out ten things you think they might not know. You can find general knowledge quizzes online, too. Maybe you could have a weekly family quiz and everyone could take it in turns to ask the questions? Or each person could find three or four questions each week so you all get a turn.

Tip: If you want people to be happy to take part, choose the questions carefully. Choose a range of topics they are interested in and make sure the questions are difficult enough (so they feel proud of getting them right) but not too difficult (so they don't get frustrated). Maybe you could offer a prize: you'll do a chore for whoever wins!

This will exercise the curiosity your brain loves and builds your own knowledge as you discover the answers for yourself.

WHAT YOU'VE LEARNT

You were already naturally curious because you're human. But now you know how to build on that natural curiosity. You're now inspired to harness curiosity to become expert at whatever you choose and to develop lots of brain areas.

Using curiosity like this is fun! You just have to focus on what you're interested in. And when you have to do something you don't enjoy – which happens to everyone – you can do it more easily when you kickstart your curiosity with my tips.

EIGHT

BE CREATIVE

THE MAIN MESSAGE

Humans are a brilliantly creative species. We don't only copy what our ancestors did: we do things differently, creating new ideas, inventions, tools and beautiful things. The brain has evolved to allow you to be creative: all you have to do is give it a chance.

WHAT YOU NEED TO KNOW

WHAT DO WE MEAN BY CREATIVE?

You can be creative in many ways. For example, you could create:

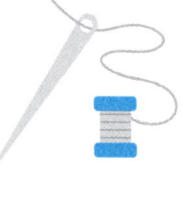

*A picture – with paint, pencil, collage,
charcoal or anything you'd like to use
A song – with or without words
A poem – rhyming or not
A story – short or long
A sculpture or model or any 3D object
The design for a piece of clothing
The design for a house, ship, plane or bridge
An invention to solve a problem
A new thought or a new way of doing something*

Ideas are often influenced by other people's creations but being creative is not copying: it's doing something of your own. You might use someone else's idea as a starting point but you make it your own in some way.

HUMANS AND CREATIVITY

Unlike other animals, humans constantly and deliberately change their environments, creating visual art, music, engineering and architecture, machines and gadgets, and poetry and stories. People create new art and designs all the time, rather than only copying their ancestors.

People enjoy talking about their creations, discussing what they like or don't like. Humans are the only creatures with brains that allow all those things.

And creativity has many uses: lots of careers involve it. But you can also enjoy creative hobbies that will make your life more fun and your brain more brilliant.

ARE SOME PEOPLE JUST MORE CREATIVE?

They might seem more creative but it's just as likely that they've had more opportunities. You can have opportunities, too, if you go looking. Remember growth mindset? Everyone is born with a brain that can be creative. Everyone can build the necessary skills, confidence and enjoyment for a brilliantly creative brain.

BRILLIANT BRAIN BOOST

Find a book or website which shows the art of these artists: Salvador Dali, Frida Kahlo, Barbara Hepworth and Pablo Picasso. They all looked for ways to create art that makes us see things in a different way.

HOW DOES BEING CREATIVE HELP YOUR BRAIN?

You know that being creative is a good idea, but what are the specific benefits for your brain?

Building networks

Creativity uses different parts of the brain, so you're growing and strengthening neural networks in lots of areas.

Self-esteem and pride

Have you ever made something and felt proud of it? If not, can you imagine how you might feel if you wrote, drew, made or designed something that turned out to be unusual, interesting, beautiful or useful? You'll get a huge sense of satisfaction. And it's fun trying!

Pleasure, fun and relaxation

You can be creative both at school and in your free time. Schoolwork often involves creativity, but you can also choose creative hobbies which might be really different. Those hobbies can be valuable ways to relax and take a break. Taking breaks is important for learning, as you'll see in Chapter Ten.

Processing negative feelings

Being creative also improves mental health by helping you process negative feelings. Many people find that writing or drawing can help when they feel distressed, sad or angry.

Improving empathy

When you create, you are often trying to identify with other people's reactions and emotions. You start to get a sense of how different people feel. The more you practise being creative, the more you practise empathy.

WHAT BRAIN PARTS DOES CREATIVITY USE?

Lots! Every type of creativity will use different areas. Here are some areas that you will use:

Prefrontal cortex

This is where you work things out and make plans. When you think about your creative idea, you use this part.

Visual areas

If you're creating something visual or even imagining what something will look like, you're using your visual areas.

Emotional areas

Creativity is a way of expressing emotions and these are processed in many areas of the brain, including parts of the limbic system.

QUESTION FROM YOU

WILL IT EVER BE POSSIBLE TO HAVE A BRAIN TRANSPLANT?

If it were possible to transplant a brain, this would really be a *body* transplant as the "person" would be the brain, with its memories. If a new brain was put in your head, you wouldn't be you. Whole brain transplants will probably stay in fiction. However, a partial brain transplant might be possible one day, to replace a damaged brain part.

JAMES ASKED

HOW TO USE
THIS KNOWLEDGE

I have lots of ideas to exercise your natural creativity. Some cost money but others don't. Some are easy from the start and others take more practice. Try as many as you can. You might discover a brilliant new skill, passion or hobby!

Before you try any of the ideas:

1. Always follow safety instructions for materials you use.

2. Creative projects can be messy! Plan ahead, protect surroundings, know in advance how to clear up a spillage and have cleaning materials handy.

3. You'll have more fun and success if you start by searching online for tips. Preparation and planning pay off!

EXPRESS YOURSELF IN VISUAL ART

Don't worry about whether anyone will see your art – just have fun!

Open your mind

Don't only think of drawing and painting. There's collage, quilling, sand art, pressing flowers, tracing. You can make models and sculpture with clay or dough or wood or plaster. There are things you can do with a phone or a camera. Some art galleries have creative ideas.

What do you like?

Which styles attract you? Look at book jackets, images on websites, cartoons. Start to work out what you like to look at and then start your own creations in that style.

Look out for artists who teach

Lots of children's book artists are generous with their time and ideas. They often have challenges, competitions and free tutorials on their websites or on social media.

Use technology

There are wonderful software programs (sometimes free) for digital artwork. Look online for the most up-to-date options.

Use a craft website

There is an enormous range of craft materials, often available cheaply. Again, search online for the most popular site in your country.

Be arty with a phone

If you have a smartphone, you'll already have taken amazing photos – why not take this to a whole new level by learning tricks with lighting, angles, frames and filters? You'll find tips online.

Become a film-maker

You can make amazing videos on a smartphone. Filming with a friend gives you even more options, as you can combine two films with different angles.

Think 3D

You can also be creative by making models or sculptures. Models could be from a kit. Or you can go freehand and make whatever you want with things such as clay, wood or scrap materials.

Make useful things

Art doesn't have to be useful, but useful objects can certainly also be beautiful. Imagine you are choosing a new coat or gloves: how they look makes a difference, as well as whether they'll do their job. Here are some things you might create which could be useful and beautiful: decorated cardboard boxes, painted plant-pots, sewing, knitting, crocheting, embroidery, tapestry, quilting, jewellery, woodwork.

Make decorations for your next festival or holiday. You could save money, have fun and feel satisfied with your creations around the house. As always, searching online for inspiration will get you started. You could invite your friends round for a mass decoration-making session! You might even sell the results and raise money for a cause.

EXPRESS YOURSELF WITH WORDS

When you're thinking what to write, start with what you like to read. You don't have to write for publication: you can write for yourself or your friends. You can start a writing group and write for them. You can put your work online or print it or keep it to yourself. Many people write and never try to publish it. That's fine! Here are some ideas.

Look online

Search "young writers" and the country or language you're in and you'll find organisations or groups where young writers can hang out. Take care and beware of scams asking you to pay money to publish. Before joining a group, check with a trusted adult.

Online forums

Writing forums where young people can upload their words can be really inspiring and useful. But you need to be aware of a few risks which apply to any online writing forum:

- Find a site appropriate for your age. If you join a site for people who are older than you, you may find material that makes you uncomfortable.

- You might get upsetting feedback.

- You will be more supported if a real-life friend is on the same website with you. If something upsets either of you, talk to a trusted adult.

- Your work might be copied or you might accidentally break copyright laws yourself – ask a librarian what the rules are.

Try fan fiction

Fan fiction (when fans of a popular book or series write stories based on the characters) can be a fun way to develop writing skills and engage with readers who share the same passions. The same warnings apply as for writing forums, if you share your work online.

Write a poem or song

Poetry is one of the best ways to start expressing yourself because a poem can be very short. It doesn't have to rhyme or even have the same lengths of line. Poems can be ordinary, silly, funny, persuasive, or anything you choose. They can be beautifully descriptive or use plainer language. And some poems work as songs.

All good writers redraft their words until they are just right but when you write a poem you'll do this even more. You'll polish and polish and spend time choosing the perfect word. Lots of people like writing poems because you can spend time polishing a small number of words, rather than trying to manage thousands.

It's often better to start with non-rhyming poems as forcing the words to rhyme can make the poem less powerful. Play with language and listen to the sound and rhythm. Rap is a good way to start. Listening to the lyrics of your favourite music can also inspire you. And try turning your poem into a song by adding whatever tune fits!

EXPRESS YOURSELF WITH MUSIC

There's a huge range of ways of making and enjoying music. If it feels like music to you, it is!

Make music

If you like listening to music, you can make it, too. Music is just sounds, chosen and put together in a way that seems beautiful or meaningful or expressive. You can even make instruments! There are objects in most homes that can be used to make different sounds. You can do it with bottles filled with varying amounts of water and objects made of metal, wood, stone or anything.

Enjoy music

You don't even have to create music to express yourself with it. Just selecting the music that suits your mood allows you to channel your emotions. You can dance to music, too, to express yourself. No one has to see! Or you could join a dance class or create routines with your friends. It's good for body and brain, stretching muscles and joints and using many areas of your brain.

BE INVENTIVE

Ever had an idea and wished you could make it happen? Maybe you could. Your brain is brilliant at solving problems – have a go!

Solving a problem

Being creative often involves problem-solving. Have you ever thought, "What if this task could be made easier?" Or is there something that's irritating and needs fixing? "How could I stop my bedroom door from swinging open by itself?" Get your creative mind thinking up solutions and try them out.

3D printing

I've always thought 3D printing is twenty-first-century magic and I don't pretend to know how it works. But I do know that students have produced stunningly creative objects using this technology in school workshops. If your school has a 3D printer, what could you suggest using it for?

Planning a project or event

Maybe a charity fundraising event; something at your school; a holiday club with your friends; a film you'd like to make. Anything that involves lots of different elements and working in a team to achieve the goal.

ACTIVITY FOR THIS CHAPTER

Choose a poetry or art activity from the ideas that follow. Set aside an hour. You can play music while you work if you like.

Poetry ideas

● Pick a letter of the alphabet and spend one minute writing every word you can think of beginning with that letter. See how many you can fit into a poem of eight lines.

● Make a shape poem, where the lines create a simple shape on the page. For example, a poem about a tree with a tree shape.

● Write about something you love, perhaps your favourite food, place, or person. Start by jotting words or phrases about why you love that thing. Then select some to write a poem.

● Write a poem where each line starts with a particular letter to spell a whole word. For example:

> **Crocodile hides in the water**
> **Rushes rustle as the deer steps near**
> **O is the shape of the people's mouths**
> **Crocodile slowly slithers closer**
> **O is the shape of the people's mouths**
> **Doomed is the deer, the people fear**
> **Ignorant is the deer, the people sneer**
> **Lightning fast is the deer disappearing**
> **Escaping to live another day**

Art ideas

Using any type of art you like, illustrate or express one of these ideas:

- Fear
- In my mirror
- A dream
- Tomorrow
- Old age
- Green
- A new leaf
- The colour of music
- Space
- Wonderland
- Shadow
- Sweet

WHAT YOU'VE LEARNT

You have discovered new possibilities for your brilliant brain! Fun things which stretch and build the brain areas which make us human. You don't have to end up in a job which people call creative but you can still express yourself and be creative throughout your life.

Being creative is enjoyable and relaxing; it boosts self-esteem; and it produces things that can be enjoyed by other people and, most importantly, you. And there's so much to choose from: you could spend your life trying out different ways to be creative and you still wouldn't have done everything!

NINE

LOVE BOOKS

THE MAIN MESSAGE

If you already love reading, the good news is that it's brilliant for your brain! If you don't, or if you believe it's difficult or boring, I will show you how it's much easier and more fun than you think. Reading opens and grows your mind.

WHAT YOU NEED TO KNOW

WHAT BENEFITS DOES READING BRING TO YOUR BRAIN?

Lots! Reading, especially reading for pleasure, has been shown to improve:

Vocabulary

Knowledge of the world

Empathy

Understanding different lives

Self-understanding

Mental health

Stress levels

Self-esteem

School results

This does not mean that if you don't read you can't improve those things. But people who read for pleasure have advantages.

Different types of book might give different benefits, just like different foods having different nutrients. So, it's sensible to read a variety, just as you'd eat a variety of food!

BRILLIANT BRAIN BOOST

Readaxation is a word I invented. It means "reading deliberately to relax". Lots of research shows that reading is a brilliant way for many people to relax. You can test it out! Download and print the Readaxation Quiz on my website. Or just follow these instructions for seven nights in a row:

1. Get ready for reading in bed.
2. Record on a scale of zero to four how stressed you feel at this moment.
3. Then read a book you like for half an hour or more.
4. Record on a scale of zero to four how stressed you feel after reading.

Most people notice that they feel less stressed. It's not a scientific measurement but how you feel is all that matters!

YOUR BRAIN IS ALREADY BRILLIANT AT READING!

Let me show you the awesome power of your reading skills.

When I tell you, turn to the next page. When you do (not yet!) you will see a box containing an eight letter word and a row of eight numbers.

DO NOT READ the word or numbers. Got that? Do not read the word or numbers.

But don't cover the box until I say!

If you accidentally read them, try to forget what they said.

Turn the page now. Avoid reading the box but read the lines below it.

```
elephant
36278149
```

You are now on this page but you're not reading the word or numbers in the box. Well done! You are probably wondering what the point is. You'll see in a moment.

Now do this:

1. Cover the forbidden box with your hand or a piece of paper. Keep it covered until I tell you to uncover it.
2. Say the word from the box. I'm guessing you know it, because you are so good at reading that you can't not read, even though you tried not to!
3. Now say the number. I'm guessing you can't! That's because numbers aren't the same as words. They should be easier to read because they are a hundred per cent regular and you only have to learn nine symbols. But you can read words better and more automatically than numbers.

Do you agree now that you are good at reading? So good that you can't not read.

DOES IT MATTER WHAT YOU READ?

There is only one important rule: it has to be your choice, no one else's! This is reading for pleasure, not reading what someone told you to. There's a good reason why pleasure is important: if you don't enjoy something enough, you won't do it and if you don't do it, you won't become good at it. That's the point of practice, remember.

Adults often say, "Surely you don't want to read that again?" or "Can't you move on to a different author?" Of course, it's good to stretch ourselves and experience new challenges, but the main thing with reading is to do it. Reading for pleasure needs to be whatever gives *you* pleasure, not someone else.

Everyone's different. Some people love learning facts; or escaping into a fantasy world; some like to be scared or to laugh; some want to be surprised; others to feel safe. It's your choice.

QUESTION FROM YOU

MARTHA ASKED

IS OUR BRAIN THE SAME SIZE AS OUR FISTS PUT TOGETHER?

It depends how big your fists are! Which partly depends on how old you are. A full-size human brain could be very roughly the size of two average adult fists.

DOES IT MATTER IF YOU READ AN EBOOK OR PRINT?

No and yes. Reading on screen and paper are both reading and both can be pleasurable. Some people prefer one to the other. There are advantages to each.

Here are some things to know before you choose.

Disadvantages of screens:

☑ When people are tested on what they read, they more often do slightly less well if they read on screen, compared to print. This applies more with difficult text, so reading print might be better when it's something you're finding hard to understand.

☑ Many people find it harder to "get into" something properly on screen. But if *you* can read an ebook easily, that's no problem!

☑ Young readers who only read on screens are less likely to say they enjoy reading than those who read print or both.

☑ Screens can make concentration harder because of distractions: adverts, moving images, notifications, hyperlinks.

☑ If you read before sleep, the light from some screens can make it harder to sleep. (See page 76.)

☑ Many printed books are beautiful, with gorgeous covers and rich illustrations. Humans are wired to love beautiful things! So a print book might encourage or remind you to read it, which you won't get from an ebook.

Advantages of screens:

- ✉ You can often change the font size and background colour, which is extremely helpful for some people.

- ✉ You can look up a meaning or pronunciation. (Although that can also be a distraction.)

- ✉ You can store hundreds of books and carry them easily.

- ✉ Ebooks are usually cheaper and sometimes free to own. (Make sure you have a legal copy, though.)

- ✉ People don't know what you're reading so you won't be judged.

If you like ebooks and find it easy to become really engaged in them, they are definitely a good idea. Neither ebooks nor print are "better" – use whichever you like!

ARE AUDIO BOOKS JUST AS GOOD?

Audio books use some different skills and brain areas, but they are a very useful way to enjoy a book. It can be relaxing listening to a book. And an audio book allows you to enjoy books that are longer or more difficult than you usually choose. You can listen on a long car journey where reading might make you feel sick, and listen before sleep without needing a light.

But reading words is an incredibly important skill. If you think about normal daily life, you'll realise that text is everywhere, and if we can't read it easily we miss opportunities. Being a fluent reader makes many jobs easier and gives us confidence and self-esteem. Besides, most books are not available in audio format. Reading uses far more brain areas than listening so reading is giving your brain a bigger workout, too.

So, audio books are a great choice sometimes, but don't let your brain miss out on its essential reading experiences. Pick up a book and dive into the wonderful words on the page.

DOES WATCHING THE SCREEN VERSION OF A BOOK BOOST YOUR BRAIN?

A film or TV programme uses fewer brain areas so it doesn't exercise your brain as much as reading. There's nothing wrong with them: they can be useful and enjoyable but they don't replace reading.

Screen versions don't engage your imagination because everything is shown to you. When you read or listen to the words of a book your brain creates the scene itself. And the reading experience is more personal, inside your head.

But screen versions let you experience stories you wouldn't otherwise read. They can be mind-opening, too. They are not the same for your brain as reading, but they are fun and can be useful ways of learning, too. They all help build your brilliant brain!

HOW TO USE
THIS KNOWLEDGE

Whether you're a keen reader already or not, take a look at these ideas. I believe there's something for everyone.

FIND YOUR STYLE OF BOOK

This activity will help you find books to love. Here's a list of things that we can get from books. Pick between two and four that you would personally enjoy:

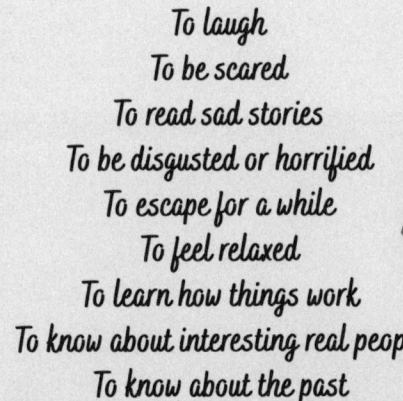

To laugh
To be scared
To read sad stories
To be disgusted or horrified
To escape for a while
To feel relaxed
To learn how things work
To know about interesting real people
To know about the past
To know about inventions or science or space
To read about people like me

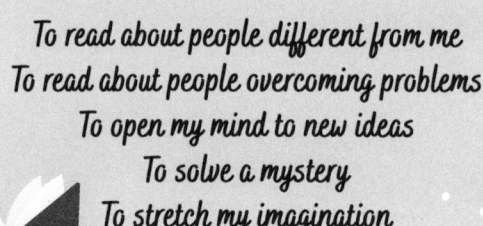

To read about people different from me
To read about people overcoming problems
To open my mind to new ideas
To solve a mystery
To stretch my imagination

Pick a book that might give you those things. Ask a librarian, bookseller, any adult who likes books and they'll give you ideas. Or use an online book-choosing tool. It's a good idea to pick several books, in case you don't enjoy the first one you pick.

Choose where, when and for how long you'll read. Get comfortable and make sure you won't be disturbed. Now dive into your chosen book.

Did you get any of the effects you wanted? Hooray! If not, choose another book. And see which of these next tips might help.

155

Set easy goals

Easy books can be just as brilliant, exciting, fun, mind-opening and good as any other book. "Easy" is different for everyone. I don't find it easy to read a graphic novel but you might.

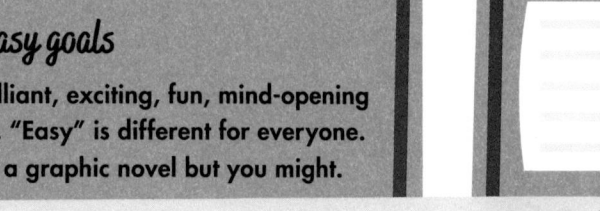

Choose books that are right for you

Think about your interests and base your choices on them. If you have a sporting hero or hobby, choose books about that. If you want to read about werewolves or murderers, do! If all your friends rave about a particular book but you don't like it, that's fine. Not everyone has to like the same books.

You don't have to finish a book!

You don't have to finish a book you're not enjoying. There are far too many wonderful books to waste time reading the wrong one!

Love your school library

A school library is a brilliant place to become a great reader. School librarians know more about choosing books than anyone. Tell yours what kind of book you're looking for. And never be afraid to say you find reading difficult or boring: the librarian will love that you're trying.

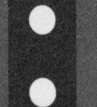

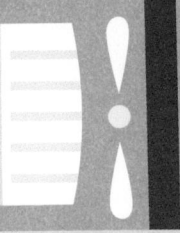

Love your public library

Public libraries are open in school holidays, too, and have staff trained to help people of all ages find books to love. Books are FREE in all libraries!

Join or start a book group

This could be at school or outside. If there isn't one already, your school librarian might start one. It's a brilliant way to make reading a social activity and get new ideas about books. You can find online groups, too. Look for one for your age group so you have more fun and feel comfortable.

Try graphic novels

Lots of readers find that graphic novels bring books to life. Some classic novels have been retold as graphic novels.

Choose non-fiction

You might prefer true stories or factual books. Think of a topic, event or person that interests you, and ask a librarian to suggest a gripping book about your topic.

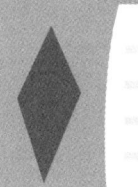

BRILLIANT BRAIN BOOST

Take any book you've read and design a different cover for it. Give it a whole new style. You can do this on paper or screen. Show your school librarian. Maybe even send it to the author!

Join a fun challenge

Reading challenges are usually in the long school holidays, and organised by your school, library or a national reading organisation. They can be fun and motivating and there are usually lots of book suggestions.

Look forward to bedtime

You know (from page 75) how important a bedtime routine is and reading is one of the best things in that routine. It helps you relax.

Ebooks or print – the choice is yours

You learnt on page 150 about the differences. If you choose ebooks, make sure you have notifications turned off. And if you're reading in bed in the evening, have the screen brightness set for night-time.

SPECIALLY FOR DYSLEXIC READERS

If you have dyslexia, there are things that can make your brain respond better to written words. Sometimes it's the colour of the paper or the choice of font. Sometimes it's the style of writing. Some publishers specialise in publishing books that fit these preferences. Look out for books described as "Hi-Lo" – high interest but lower difficulty – so you can easily read things that interest you. Don't make it hard for yourself – it's meant to be pleasure!

ACTIVITY FOR THIS CHAPTER

Here's a fun way of finding a book that you'll love.

1. Which of these things would you like to see in a story?

An alien or monster
A ghostly or spooky happening
A cruel villain
An annoying brother or sister
Magic
An incredible fantasy world
A difficult family situation
Friendship trouble
Romance
A young person who becomes a hero
A friendship between a character and a dog or horse

2. Ask your friends (and teachers, librarians, parents) to see if you can all think of books where these things happen.

3. Now ask your librarian for some recommendations of any other books that feature these things. Make a list of books that look appealing.

4. Pick one from the list and start reading!

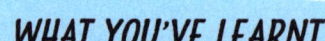

WHAT YOU'VE LEARNT

Books bring amazing benefits for your brain. They do obvious things like building knowledge and vocabulary and ideas. And less obvious ones like boosting self-esteem, mental health and reaction to stress.

Lots of people love reading but not everyone does, just as some people love physical exercise and others only do it because they have to. But, among all the millions of books, there are some for everyone to enjoy. You just need to find the ones for you. There are plenty of people and websites to help and a whole world of books out there. Authors wrote them for you and your brilliant brain to love! Books change lives and brains. Let them change yours!

TEN

TAKE BREAKS

THE MAIN MESSAGE

Your brain won't be so brilliant if you make it work hard all the time. Of course, work is important. You know that. But taking breaks and having fun helps your brain flourish. Then you can work well and enjoy your life.

WHAT YOU NEED TO KNOW

WHAT EXACTLY IS A BREAK?

Taking a break could be switching to something else, a different task or piece of work, for example. Or it could be doing something enjoyable and coming back refreshed. Both help your brain.

DOES IT MATTER WHAT YOU DO IN THE BREAK?

There are two especially brain-friendly things you could do in these breaks:

1. Physical exercise
2. Face-to-face social activity

Your break activity can be anything you enjoy but it's also a really good idea to get away from your desk and your screen. Although playing a computer game is fun and can be relaxing, you're still sitting at a screen, which isn't the best choice.

BREAKS HELP YOUR LEARNING

Suppose you have three bits of homework: learning spellings, solving a maths problem and finding five facts about the moon. Your brain will usually do the second and third tasks better if you have a break after learning your spellings. And you'll be more likely to remember the spellings! Magic!

CAN YOU HAVE TOO MANY BREAKS?

Yes! Too many breaks might stop you finishing your work. It's important to spend enough time on whatever you need to do. When you're "in the zone", you don't want to spoil that flow.

But if you're bored or you don't like the work, it can be tempting to take too many breaks. Try to spot when you're doing that and push yourself to get stuck into a task.

Listen to your body and mind: if you feel refreshed and ready to tackle your tasks, you've had enough of a break. If you feel tired and your mind isn't ready to work, you might need more breaks. Sometimes you do need to push yourself, but don't overdo it.

BRILLIANT BRAIN FACT

The best time for a break is often before you finish a piece of work, not after! If you leave the work for a bit, your brain carries on processing. Then when you come back to it, you'll have an even better chance of understanding and remembering.

RELAXATION HELPS YOUR BRAIN

Just as you need great food, sleep and exercise, you also need enough relaxation in your day. It helps your brain. Without relaxation, you won't have good well-being and then your brain can't do its best.

LAUGHTER IS GOOD FOR YOU

When you laugh, your brain releases endorphins, those natural chemicals that make you feel better. See if you can find something to make you laugh at least once a day.

relaxation

better well-being

success

even better well-being

WHAT ACTUALLY HAPPENS IN YOUR BRAIN WHEN YOU THINK?

Energy! Electrical currents whizz along pathways. A thought is really only electricity plus chemicals called **neurotransmitters** that help it travel. If you've had a thought (or one like it) before, the message will travel along neural networks you've already made. If it's a new thought, it will make new networks.

QUESTION FROM YOU

MATILDA & LUCY ASKED

TWO TYPES OF STRESS

You learnt about the stress response on page 12. But there are two different ways of feeling stressed. Each needs different relaxation activities. You might feel physical signs of anxiety. For example, you might experience:

✿ Breathing and heart beating faster than usual

✿ Sweaty skin

✿ The feeling of "butterflies in your stomach"

✿ Feeling sick or dizzy

✿ A headache, stomach ache or tight chest

Or your stress might be a big worry on your mind. You might:

✿ Be thinking about a test or competition or speaking in front of your class

✿ Have something upsetting going on at home

✿ Be worried about something you've done

✿ Have a friendship that's going badly

✿ Be scared of something bad happening in the future

Depending on which type of stress you feel, you need either calming or distracting activities to help you relax. Ideas for both are coming up!

HOW TO USE
THIS KNOWLEDGE

Lots of people don't need advice about how to relax but lots do. Perhaps you're the sort of person who finds it difficult to switch off. Maybe you're feeling low, which makes it hard to have fun. Or perhaps you just want some more ideas. Read on!

CHOOSE YOUR RELAXATION

You'll see great ideas on the opposite page, but here are some general points to help you choose:

Choose a variety of physical and mental activities. Try not to do one thing for too long. For example, computer games are fine for a short time but then do something different. Do what YOU enjoy. If you need to be alone, be alone.

On page 165, I said that there were two different ways of feeling stressed. If you're feeling physically anxious, you need something calming. If you've got a big worry, you need something distracting. Here are ideas for each:

CALMING

A breathing exercise such as "belly-breathing"

A bath or shower

Lying on the grass or a beach

Gentle swimming or stretching exercises

Stroking a pet

Anything easy and relaxing

DISTRACTING

An exciting video game

Watching something exciting on TV or online

Playing or watching sport

Anything you have to concentrate on

Reading a book that engages you

BRILLIANT BRAIN BOOST

When you've spent time on one thing, it can be good to switch to a different type of activity. If you've been spending a lot of time revising for a test and you stop to play football or bake a cake, when you come back you'll find the work easier. Your brain has had a boost.

CHECK YOUR BREATHING

Anxiety affects your breathing. You can test whether you're breathing in a calm or anxious way. Here's how:

1. Sit comfortably.

2. Put one hand flat on your stomach and the other just below your throat, flat on your upper chest.

3. As you breathe, which hand moves more?

If your lower hand moves more, you seem relaxed. The upper hand moving more suggests anxiety or alertness, which is tiring after a time. The next page shows you how to calm your breathing whenever you want.

BELLY-BREATHING AND RELAXATION

Now you can do belly-breathing! Focus on making your belly expand as you breathe in and soften as you breathe out. Here's how you can use this to relax your whole body:

1. Sit or lie comfortably. Try to make sure you won't be disturbed.

2. Spend around 30 seconds focusing on belly-breathing: slowly breathe in, letting your belly expand and loosen, and then breathe out. Each out-breath should be a bit longer than the in-breath.

3. Now, focus on your toes and feet. Make them relax. Feel them become heavier with each breath. Keep belly-breathing.

4. Then focus on your calves, knees, thighs, and slowly all the way up your body. Relax the muscles in each part of your body. When you reach your neck, go even more slowly, focusing on the back of your neck, your scalp, and down to your forehead, eyes, cheeks, jaw, mouth. Feel each part soften.

Your breathing and heart rate will slow and you should feel more relaxed. Stay doing this for as long as you want to. You can also do this to help you fall asleep.

MINDFULNESS

Mindfulness is a type of meditation. It asks you to stop rushing about – physically and mentally – and focus on tiny details of what you're doing. Although you need lessons to learn it properly, there are some simple ways anyone can try:

Instead of eating your food fast without thinking, slow down and enjoy the tastes, notice the feel in your mouth, the smell, texture.

Look at each hair on your arm.

Just listen. How many different sounds can you hear?

Take a lemon or apple and focus on the smell, the feel of the skin, the weight.

Think about all the feelings in your body, your skin, your face, your fingers.

When walking to school, notice the trees, houses, people.

Pick a single flower and try drawing it.

Pick up a leaf or flower and look at each mark on it.

SHORT BREAKS

When you're working, it's good to take regular breaks. Set an hourly alert to remind you to step away from work and spend five to ten minutes on any of the following.

Thirsty? Pep up a glass of water with ice and a slice of fruit.

Hungry? Choose a snack: nuts; cheese or egg sandwich; fruit; raisins; cheese on cracker.

Is there a five-minute chore you've been putting off? Do it! Make your bed; fold your clothes; tidy your floor.

Dance to a favourite song.

Get fresh air with a short walk.

Go outside and breathe deeply, feeling the air expand your lungs. Relax your stomach as you breathe. Be proud of the work you've been doing.

Here are lots of relaxing ideas. Some only take a few minutes. Can you think of others?

Breathe deeply, walk, bath or shower, bake or cook, make something, lie on the grass or a beach, listen to music, play sport, watch sport, read, draw or doodle, smell your favourite smell, stroke a pet, laugh, play any game, make a birthday card, swim, do yoga, go to the park, dance, tidy your room (really!), plant seeds, make a daisy chain, create a play or song, look at something beautiful and think about it properly, eat an apple while noticing every mouthful.

HAVE A LAUGH

On page 164 you learnt why laughter is good for your brain. But it's difficult if you're feeling down. Or perhaps you're naturally quite a serious person. How can you get the laughter you need?

Everyone's different. Think about what makes you laugh: certain books, videos, comedians, TV shows? On YouTube you'll find babies eating lemons, goats screaming like humans, talking dogs and many more funny videos. Build a collection to go to when you want to laugh.

Something you might not have heard of is laughter yoga. Check it out! There are exercises to make you laugh. Ask your teacher if they'd like to try it with your class, too!

BRILLIANT BRAIN BOOST

Even smiling triggers those endorphins. Try a big smile now and hold it for a few seconds. Use your whole face, not just your mouth. What do you notice? Do you feel strangely lighter?

ACTIVITY FOR THIS CHAPTER

Make a poster of your favourite relaxing activities. Decorate it however you choose. You'll see some ideas below.

Pin it to your wall. The point is that, when you're stressed, you forget how to relax. This poster reminds you.

WHAT YOU'VE LEARNT

Taking breaks is a very important way of helping your brilliant brain work well. A break helps refresh you when you've been working or thinking and it helps you process what you learn. Having enough time for relaxation, enjoyment and fun is really important. It's not a luxury but necessary for well-being. You need to choose the right activity to suit your situation. And you need to laugh!

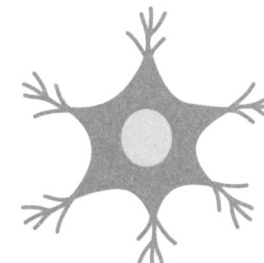

HOW TO LEARN MORE

My website has masses of information about how you can look after your brain and explore the science. As well as all my books for young people, there are lots of materials for schools and families to use. Tell your teachers and parents! You'll find a page especially for this book, too, with lots of links and downloads, including printable postcards and posters.

Visit www.nicolamorgan.com, choose the Books section and scroll to *Ten Ways to Build a Brilliant Brain*.

YOUR BRAIN IS BRILLIANT

Did you start this book thinking that you can't control much about your brain? I hope you now see that there's a lot you can control. Your brain was already brilliant but you now have the tools to make it even better.

You now know how to take all the opportunities you find, to build your brilliant brain day by day, step by step, neuron by neuron.

No one can control everything but we each need to focus on what we can control – and there's a lot of that. This book has given you ten things you can do to build your own most brilliant brain:

Building neural connections
Eating wonderful food
Moving your body
Getting the best sleep
Enjoying friendships
Bouncing back when bad things happen
Being curious
Stretching your creative powers
Escaping into the books you choose
Relaxing and having fun

Your brilliant brain is in your hands. Look after it and it will look after you. You have the power! Have fun using it!

   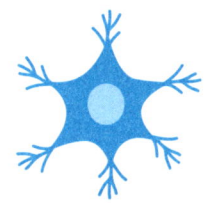

BRAINY WORDS

Dendrites – The branches that grow from neurons, enabling the cells to form connecting networks and communicate with each other.

Dopamine – I call this neurotransmitter (see below) the YES chemical and it's a crucial part of the brain's reward system, making us feel good.

Endorphins – A group of hormones (a type of chemical) released in the brain and nervous system to reduce stress and pain. Sometimes called the brain's "happy chemicals".

Mindset – A way of thinking or set of beliefs. Mindsets often change and are affected by people we spend time with and listen to. Mindsets can be positive or negative.

Neuron – Also called a "nerve cell", there are between 85 and 100 billion neurons in your brain and spinal cord. Neurons communicate with each other to allow a person to do any mental or physical action.

Neurotransmitters – Brain chemicals that help messages travel between neurons. There are many different neurotransmitters, each with different jobs.

Process – When we say the brain processes information, we mean that it receives and deals with information, moving it to the correct brain area. While you're awake, you're seeing, hearing, smelling, touching, reading, receiving countless bits of information and doing something with it: deciding, fearing, liking, avoiding, remembering, repeating.

Wired – How neurons are connected together. First, your brain is wired in a human way. Second, your brain is wired in ways that are individual to you, so how you think, feel and behave is not exactly the same as for someone else. Also, your brain keeps changing – re-wiring. Everything you experience changes bits of wiring in your brain.

  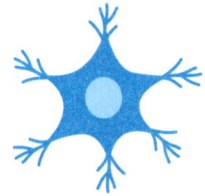